Living Deliberately

Copyright © Hrvoje Butković, 2011. All rights reserved. No part of this book may be reproduced or transmitted in any form or by any means, electronic or mechanical, including photocopying, recording, or by any information storage and retrieval system, without permission in writing from the publisher.

Millennial Mind Publishing
An imprint of American Book Publishing
5442 So. 900 East, #146
Salt Lake City, UT 84117-7204
www.american-book.com
Printed in the United States of America on acid-free paper.

Living Deliberately

Designed by Troy D. O'Brien, design@american-book.com

Publisher's Note: American Book Publishing relies on the author's integrity of research and attribution; each statement has not been investigated to determine if it has been accurately made. The author and publisher specifically disclaim any responsibility for any liability, loss, or risk, personal or otherwise, which is incurred as a consequence, directly or indirectly, of the use and application of any of the contents of this book. In such situations where medical, legal, or other professional services may apply, please seek the advice of such professionals directly.

ISBN-13: 978-1-58982-771-4
ISBN-10: 1-58982-771-6

Library of Congress Cataloging-in-Publication Data
Butkovic, Hrvoje.
Living deliberately / Hrvoje Butkovic.
  p. cm.
ISBN-13: 978-1-58982-771-4
ISBN-10: 1-58982-771-6
  1. Conduct of life. 2. Life. 3. Decision making. 4. Awareness I. Title.
BJ1521.B925 2010
158.1--dc22
                    2010035642

Special Sales: These books are available at special discounts for bulk purchases. Special editions, including personalized covers, excerpts of existing books, and corporate imprints, can be created in large quantities for special needs. For more information e-mail info@american-book.com.

Living Deliberately

Hrvoje Butković

Table of Contents

Introduction 11

Part 1: What Is Deliberate Living? 17

Key Concepts Pertaining to Deliberate Living 19
    The Definition 20
    Compatibility with Belief Systems 21
    Usefulness 22
    Looking Beyond 24
The Underlying Life Philosophy 27
    The Approach to Life 28
    The Role of Circumstances 29
    The Role of other People 31
Criticism of the Underlying Life Philosophy 33
    Intensity 34
    Seriousness 35
    Self-centeredness 36
    Difficult Circumstances 37

Living Deliberately

Part 2: How Is Deliberate Living Achieved?............39

The Placement of Responsibility..................................41
   Assuming Personal Responsibility........................42
   The Scope of Responsibility....................................43
Cultivating Awareness of Our Conduct........................49
   Multitasking..50
   Chattering...55
   Automatically Responding to Circumstances........57
   Experiencing Pain..60
Identifying the Consequences of Our Conduct..........65
   Consequences as Feelings..66
   What Is the Self?...68
   Distinguishing between Thoughts and Feelings....71
   Resolving Apparent Contradictions.......................74
   Overcoming False Internalized Beliefs..................76
Evaluating the Consequences of Our Conduct..........81
   The Value of Questions...82
   Analyzing Straightforwardly Emotional Situations......86
   Analyzing Ambiguously Emotional Situations.....87
   Analyzing Unemotional Situations........................90
   Evaluating Predictable Consequences...................91
   Dealing with Conflicting Feelings..........................92
   The Lure of Rationalization...................................94
Expanding Our Knowledge Base..................................97
   From Theory..98
   From Observing Plants...101
   From Observing Animals......................................104
   From Observing Children.....................................105
   From Observing Adults...107
   From Observing People from other Cultures.....109
   From Imagination..113

- From Inspiration 116
- The Prudence of Discernment 118
- Tying Knowledge to Circumstances 123
  - Knowledge of Circumstantial Potential 124
  - Changing Circumstances 126
  - Empathy 127
  - Trial and Error 132
  - Projection 135
- Experimenting with Beliefs 139
  - The Nature of Beliefs 140
  - Acquisition of Beliefs 141
  - Making Peace with Contradictions 144
  - Purposefully Adopting Beliefs 145
- Putting It All Together 153
  - The Role of the Past 154
  - The Role of the Future 155
  - The Role of the Present 156
- When Things Fall Apart 163
  - The Importance of Intention 164
  - Not Accomplishing Tasks 166
  - Misunderstanding Cause and Effect 169
  - Choosing Unworthy Goals 170
  - Mastering Failure 173

Part 3: What Are the Effects of Living Deliberately? ... 179

- The Difficulty of Pursuing Deliberate Living 181
  - Going It Alone 182
  - Fear of Crises 184
  - Fear of the Future 186
  - Frustration, Sadness, and Despair 187
- The Value of Attaining Deliberate Living 193

- Not Getting Hurt 194
- Release of Judgment 195
- Conscious Evolution 198
- Transcendence of Rules and Regulations 200
- The Basis of Morality 202

Likely Criticism 207
- Excessive Change 208
- Lack of Emotions 209
- Lack of Accountability for Mistakes 210
- Lack of Sensitivity in Painful Situations 211
- Non-conformance 212
- Living in a Dream World 214

In a Nutshell 217
- Subject Overview 218
- Generic Knowledge Base 221
- Personalized Knowledge Base 223
- Beliefs 225
- Decision Process 227

In Closing 231

Where to from here? 235
- Acquiring Further Insights 235
- Living the Insights 237
- Social Activism 238

Summary: Quick Reference 241

Acknowledgments 243

List of Examples

Steven's response to a forest fire 30
Sally's response to her disapproving parents 31
Elizabeth's drinking habits 50, 52
Brad's driving habits 53, 83
Dave's IT career 54, 119
Mary's ironing habits 55, 56
Michelle's weekly bridge game 58, 59
Claire's and Denise's coffee shop business 60, 62
Jim's reconnaissance mission 70
Nick's reckless driving 72
Harry's upbringing 74, 75, 77, 78
Helen's witnessing of an execution 86
Judy's abusive relationship 88, 89
Terence's tax return 90, 95
Anne's jogging 91
Jeremy's handling of difficult people 99
Melissa's love of her enemies 100
Sandra's vegetable garden 102, 103, 134
Eric's dog 104
Janet's nature documentary 105

Warren's son's angry outburst 106
Cathy's daughter's carefree playing 107
Sonja's smiling at strangers 108
Jennifer's dreams of fame 109
Durable vs. recyclable construction 111
Babemba tribe's treatment of wrongdoers 112
Melissa's response to a water shortage 113
Shaun's life as a factory worker 114
John's encounter with a beggar 115, 124, 136, 137
Alec's gym routine 117
Claire's disposal of excess food 126
Jessica's attempt to tie her shoe laces 128
Henry's family gathering 131
Charles' shower in the dark 132
Robert's environmental concerns 143
Nancy's treatment of other people as herself 147
Kyle's conversion campaigns 149
Rachel's rebound 156
Tanya's son's wall art 157, 158
Mark's abandonment of stranded strangers 159
Gary's friend's abusive relationship 165
Sarah's parenting habits 169
Harold's banking career 171
Marvin's computer games 174
Adhering to the speed limit 200
The morality of the death penalty 203

Introduction

This book is my personal journey towards deliberate living. It started in 2003, when I became aware of the concepts while reading the first Conversations with God book. As the realization sank in, the process began to crystallize. Once it did, it took off with surprising speed. At the time of this writing, I am still very much engaged in it, and there's no sight of the finish line.

I decided to write this book in 2007. Since then, I've been collecting material that I thought might be suitable for inclusion in this book, both from my personal experiences and from the experiences of others I knew. My goal was to convey the subject matter as clearly as I could while staying away from overly technical and esoteric discussions and keeping the material relevant to our daily lives. I did my best to use neutral terminology; it is my impression that spirituality is easily hindered by being conveyed in religious terms because this gives it an other-worldly quality that is divorced from our ordinary lives.

The reason I wrote this book is to share the insights that I have gathered on my life journey. I'm quite certain that they are not new, but have been discovered by other people who have walked this path before me. Still, it may be useful to share them again, in the particular format that I have chosen to use.

The book is intended to be a bridge between three distinct categories of books that I've encountered on my journey. The first one is self-help books – books that have been written to provide us with guidance regarding specific aspects of our daily lives. My experience with these kinds of books has been that they tend to present the conclusions that the author has reached on the basis of his life experience, in the hope that the readers will use them to fast-track their growth. The advice that they offer can be very effective at making use of these conclusions, at least to the extent that the reader can relate to them. However, it can be difficult to understand how these conclusions were derived or identify their place in a larger context, which makes it difficult to extend to new situations. Lacking this understanding, the reader may struggle to develop beyond the level of growth that the author has already attained.

The second category of books is popular works that are rooted in ancient philosophical and religious traditions, particularly Eastern ones. They tend to focus on a single element – such as mindfulness – and provide a comprehensive guide of how to achieve it and list its benefits. Instead of merely offering conclusions, they explain to the reader how to master the material. Unfortunately, what they generally don't do is place their subject matter in the overall context of the living of one's life so that the reader can get a good sense of where it fits in.

The third category of books can be described as mystical books – books that wrestle with the matter of ultimate reality and enlightenment. Because much of this material cannot be effectively expressed with words, they inevitably resort to describing the various techniques that the reader can use to experience for herself the reality that they describe. In so doing, they hope that the reader will acquire a shared frame of reference with which to make sense of the material that is given, as well as extend it by continued practice. What I find lacking in this approach is an indication of how it relates to ordinary social living. It is as if the knowledge and experience of higher realities automatically removes all obstacles from our mundane lives or renders living in the world unimportant, regardless of our background, beliefs, and level of development.

This book attempts to bring the three together. It goes beyond the conclusions offered by self-help literature to show the readers how to derive principles for themselves. It expands the focus of traditional religious books to identify the place of their subject matter in the larger life context. It extends the mystical literature to show how its findings can be used to enhance daily living.

The book makes no attempt to provide exhaustive analysis of the material that it covers. This material is treated more thoroughly in other specialized works written by experts on a particular subject. Rather, it aims to serve as an introductory text whose goal is to provide wide coverage of the relevant material and show how all of it comes together. Hopefully this will enable the reader to understand where individual insights fit into the living of one's life and know what topics to explore in greater depth.

In concrete terms, the nature of this advice differs in two important respects. Firstly, it tries to mold the subject matter into a cohesive whole instead of presenting disjointed tips on how to live one's life. It does so by developing a simple life philosophy and illustrating how it can be used to derive guidance in a wide variety of situations.

Secondly, the advice that it gives is not prescriptive. It does not instruct us on what we should think, say, or do in any particular situation. Even though it presents many examples of real-life circumstances, it shies away from reaching conclusions about their protagonists, and it avoids generalizing the conclusions that it does reach. A person who reads the book in search of these kinds of answers will in all likelihood be disappointed.

What the book does do is explain the process of decision-making itself. It describes various factors that influence it and uses examples to illustrate them and place them in their proper context. This approach reflects my view of personal growth. It is a process that can be hampered or assisted, but not eliminated or short-circuited. Acquisition of external answers is frequently an attempt to short-circuit it. This can offer us temporary reprieve when the same situation presents itself again, but circumstances that we typically face are far too rich and diverse for this to offer lasting benefit.

A more robust approach is to master the ability of deriving answers for ourselves. This is what the book seeks to assist with. If successful, it will leave the reader with as much work to do as before, but work that should proceed faster and more smoothly. It will enable the reader to arrive at his own answers, understand why and how these answers were derived and improve on them with the aid of life experience. When external answers are obtained, he will likewise be able to dissect them, understand why and how they work, their strong and weak points, and ways to improve them.

The basic structure of the book is to briefly state concepts and approaches and then illustrate them with examples. I have tried to give the subject matter fair treatment. Even though I see great value in the concepts and methods that are discussed, I have done my best to highlight considerable difficulties that they entail and suggest ways of overcoming them.

Each chapter ends with a short summary. Its purpose is to highlight the central themes that were discussed in the chapter. I've phrased them in question format in an effort to stimulate introspection and discourage readers from falling into the habit of accepting the answers that I've given.

It is important to realize that the book presents a particular way of looking at our lives, a filter through which we can interpret our experience, and a guideline according to which we can conduct ourselves. We should be careful not to mistake this filter for the truth and use it to invalidate other filters that can be used for this purpose, no matter how well we may find it to work.

Conversely, if we find that it conflicts with our experience, we should discard this filter in favor of others. Several others are mentioned in the book at points in the discussion where they can be easily contrasted with the main approach. If we do discard it, we should be careful not to require others to do the same.

Finally, I must acknowledge that I am very far from having all the answers on the subject. This is a journey that I've only been engaged in for a few years and, to date, do not see the end of. The criteria for including material in this book had to do with its usefulness rather than completeness. As such, the content of the book is undeniably a work in progress and does not represent the final word on the subject. Nevertheless, I hope that reading it will be informative and rewarding for the people who undertake doing so. It has certainly been rewarding to write.

Part 1:
What Is Deliberate Living?

Key Concepts Pertaining to Deliberate Living

"We can only be said to be alive in those moments when our hearts are conscious of our treasures."

Thornton Wilder

This book brings together insights and techniques from seemingly disparate fields that, when put into practice, give rise to a state of being that I can only describe as vibrantly and authentically alive. Explaining what those insights are, how they complement one another and how to make effective use of them is what the bulk of the book is about.

Before we can explore the intricacies of deliberate living and how to put it into practice, however, we need to devote some time to seeing just what I mean by the term, as well as introducing the concepts that are associated with it. The laying of this groundwork is what I'll tackle first.

There is no single definition of deliberate living. Different people have different ideas of what the term means. Many of those that I've come across operate within the bounds of a rigid belief system. Such an approach is diagrammatically opposed to the one that I'm describing here. If you are aware of alternative definitions, please keep in mind that, whenever deliberate living is mentioned in this book, it refers to an approach to life that is consistent with the definition given below.

The Definition

Deliberate living is known by many names. Some people describe it as thoughtful living, in an effort to indicate how much consideration goes into the making of daily decisions. Others refer to it as conscious living, expressing the high level of awareness at which it is carried out. Still others portray it as authentic living, conveying the high amount of freedom and individuality that are its hallmarks. A few refer to it as autonomous living in an attempt to communicate its independence from social norms. All of these terms allude to a way of living that exhibits very specific characteristics.

Within the context of this book, deliberate living will be taken to mean *living life in such a way that the protagonist is aware of what she is thinking, saying, or doing, understands why she is thinking, saying, or doing it, and approves of it being thought, said, or done, for every thought, word, and action of consequence.*

There are more idealistic versions of the definition. The same requirements that are placed on thoughts, words, and actions can also be placed on feelings and beliefs. Those requirements can be made even more stringent by encompassing *all* thoughts, words, and beliefs rather than only significant ones.

This is an unreachable ideal. It is offered because it is the most worthwhile goal that I can conceive, even if it may lie beyond our reach. Fortunately, it is not necessary to achieve even the less idealistic version of the goal to derive tremendous benefit from attempting to live in this way.

The intentionality alluded to in this definition does not refer to having definite answers to concrete questions like what our vocation should be or whom we should marry. Delivering them to us is not the purpose of deliberate living. Rather, it illuminates the process by which we can arrive at the answers ourselves.

Deliberate living as defined here is also *not* a belief system; it is a state of being. Because of the evolutionary nature of our existence, it is really a progression of states of being, each more purposeful and authentic than what came before. Therefore, knowing what we are doing and why we are doing it does not constitute static information that is the object of one's striving. The knowledge itself is subject to change in line with the evolving nature of one's being.

With this in mind, perhaps the most accurate way to describe deliberate living is as a process – *a life journey that has no final destination, but where each step that we take is its own reward, one that makes the whole journey well worth taking.*

Compatibility with Belief Systems

While deliberate living is not a belief system, it does rest on a handful of beliefs. These are derived from observation and contemplation rather than faith. Because of this, deliberate living is compatible with a wide variety of belief systems, religious or otherwise. It can be pursued without leaving them behind.

What deliberate living is not compatible with is the manner in which those beliefs are often adopted. There is a tendency in our society to use externally acquired beliefs to construct a framework which we then use to guide our interaction with the world. When this interaction produces experience, as it invariably does, we seek to harmonize it with our beliefs. In this process, it is the experience that is malleable, not the beliefs.

The approach presented in this book seeks to do the opposite. It takes our experience as the foundation of our interaction with the world. It encourages us to formulate beliefs on the basis of our experience. Should the two conflict, it is the beliefs that should be malleable, not the experience. Because of this, deliberate living, as described in this book, is fundamentally incompatible with an approach to life that sets the upholding of a belief as its goal.

Usefulness

It may be asked at this point what makes deliberate living a worthwhile goal in itself? Simply put, I cannot envisage a better way to live human life. The most meaningful, purposeful, and fulfilling way to live our lives is to ascertain what makes our lives meaningful, purposeful and fulfilling, and then deliberately pursue those things.

This immediately raises another question. *What is it that adds value to our lives?* The significance of this question shouldn't be underestimated. After all, if we cannot resist the temptation to behave cruelly and deceitfully, then we have reason to suspect that other people harbor the same preference. And if we all acted on these preferences, cruelty and deceit would become the norm, giving birth to a society of our nightmares.

I must admit that I do not share this fear, even though I've encountered it on numerous occasions. The very fact that we dread these things is evidence enough for me that they do not constitute the very essence of our being. We may slip into this kind of behavior from time to time, we may struggle to kick our hurtful and destructive habits, but this is not who we wish to be. When the concern is raised, it invariably applies to those 'other people'. Those who raise it don't see themselves as having the same problem, even as they acknowledge their own failure to conduct themselves according to the same high standards.

If engaging in cruelty and deceit is who we truly wish to be, then we should rejoice at the license to adopt them and bask in the consequences that they produce. If the prospect terrifies us, perhaps our true nature isn't as bleak as it may appear at first glance. If harmful behavior is inconsistent with our preferred self-image, then we only stand to gain by setting our sights on who we wish to be and deliberately pursuing that.

Doing so is likely to place several obstacles in our way – lack of awareness of our true nature, lack of understanding of actions and their consequences, and lack of courage to put our knowledge into practice. Any one of these is sufficient enough to thwart our efforts and reduce who we wish to be to nothing more than a fantasy.

Deliberate living can overcome these hurdles. Discovering what we are doing and understanding why we are doing it will give us the awareness of our nature that we need in order to overcome the first hurdle. Learning which actions to choose so that they meet with our approval effectively overcomes the second hurdle. If we engage in this conduct enough times, we will come to appreciate the benefits that it has to offer, which will give us the resolve to choose this path with ever-increasing frequency.

Seen in this light, the potential embodied in this approach to living is immense. I do think that it has the capacity to overcome many, if not all of the personal and collective problems that have plagued us and our society for the duration of its existence.

Looking Beyond

The stage of consciousness development associated with deliberate living as described in this book represents the height of most conventional developmental theory in the field of psychology. Termed autonomous or authentic consciousness, it is characterized by authenticity in the individual's expression, instead of his inner nature being warped, suppressed or denied, as is typical of lower levels of consciousness.

Even so, this might not be the height of development that is available to us. Informed by unconventional sources, primarily mysticism, a handful of researchers have advanced theories that deal with even higher states of consciousness. The writings of Abraham Maslow and Ken Wilber on this subject are well known. Another example is Jenny Wade's *Holonomic Theory of Consciousness*, which proposes two levels that surpass the authentic one – transcendent consciousness and unity consciousness.[1]

Having never had a profound mystical experience myself, I cannot comment on what states of being are available beyond the authentic one. What I can say is that I'm sympathetic to the view of Hazrat Inayat Khan, a Sufi mystic who was the first teacher of the Sufi tradition in the United States and Eu-

---

[1] This is described in her book *Changes of Mind: A Holonomic Theory of the Evolution of Consciousness*.

rope, and who founded the Sufi Order in the West in 1910. He saw great value in using mystical insights for personal development, what he called "the perfecting of the human personality".[2]

Even if there are levels of consciousness beyond the authentic one that are available to us, it is nevertheless a crucial stage that cannot be skipped, and that most people haven't yet attained.

Summary: Questions to Ask Myself

How deliberate do I want my life to be?

What value do I see deliberate living adding to my life?

What makes my life meaningful, purposeful, or fulfilling?

---

[2] From the back cover of his book *Personality: The Art of Being and Becoming*: "The accent in his work is on making spirituality relevant to life by bringing the insights gained in mystical experience to bear on our actions, relationships and aspirations. For him, the perfecting of the human personality is the fulfillment of the purpose of existence, the fruit of the tree of life."

The Underlying Life Philosophy

*"Who am I? Who am I? Who am I?
It is the only question God ever had."*

Neale Donald Walsch

Deliberate living, as defined in the previous chapter, is too abstract to lend itself to direct implementation. We can work on the awareness of our conduct, perhaps even uncover our reasons for it, but we cannot give it our approval until we know what it is that we are trying to accomplish.

One more step is needed. We have to set our life in a particular direction. Only once we have a concrete goal to work towards can we tell whether our thoughts, words, and actions are helping us achieve it. This direction amounts to the fundamental goal of our lives, the underlying motivation that sponsors all our other goals. It cannot be derived. It can only be adopted based on what appears to be the most worthwhile way to live one's life.

Perhaps it is unfortunate that the fundamental approach to life cannot be derived, for its choice is crucial – it enables the derivation of every decision that follows. The whole of part two of this book is essentially an attempt to implement the chosen method. Part three examines the effects of following it.

Whether we are sure of which approach to follow or not, it may be a good idea to revisit the choice occasionally, after we have made a concerted effort to implement it. If it proves unable to offer guidance in certain situations, or if the consequences that it gives rise to sometimes turn out to be unpleasant, it may be time to choose again.

The Approach to Life

The approach to life that this book presents can be summarized as an attempt to answer the question *"Who am I?"* in experiential terms. In other words, we strive to answer the question by examining our experiences and deciding which ones accurately describe us and which ones do not. As we gain proficiency with this, ideally we would seek out matching experiences and keep away from those that misrepresent us. By stringing together a series of authentic experiences, we fashion our life into a statement of who we are. This allows us to both experience the truth of our being and demonstrate it to others.

In essence, the answer that we give to the question "Who am I?" is our life, as we've lived it.

This is not an attempt to argue that answering the question of who we are in an experiential manner is the inherent purpose of our life. Rather, it advocates the adoption of this purpose as a matter of voluntary choice due to the beneficial effects that this can have on our life. It is a case of trying to live our life in the most fulfilling way that we can conceive.

Whether this is indeed its purpose or not is a separate concern.

ALTERNATIVES:

Deliberate living can be accomplished by many variations on this theme. Choosing a different approach will cause us to ask ourselves different questions. These might lead us to offer different answers as to how we should live our lives, though from my interaction with people who are following these alternatives, I haven't seen a significant difference between our behavior and its effects. What differed was mostly our justification for it.

It should be noted that, if our aim is deliberate living as defined in the previous chapter, then approaches to life that set as our goal adherence to an external standard – such as being a law-abiding citizen or fulfilling our religious duty – do not constitute a viable alternative. The reason is that, whatever guideline we adopt to conduct ourselves by, it must be able to offer us guidance in every situation. This means that it must either contain all the answers, or it must be able to derive answers as the need arises. Externally formulated codes of conduct do neither. They are largely static and limited in their coverage. As such, they can contribute to our conception of how to live our lives, but they cannot define it. Even if we choose to rely on them, we will sometimes be forced to search beyond what they can offer.

The Role of Circumstances

The cornerstone of this approach to living is to view each set of circumstances as a context within which we can express ourselves or as material from which we can fashion representative experience. We can think of them as a palette that we use to paint a self-portrait on the canvas of our lives. It is through the circumstances that we encounter that we add detail to our experiential self-image. The richer and more diverse the circumstances, the greater the range of colors with which we paint and the more breathtaking the end result.

How beautiful this portrait turns out to be depends primarily on the beauty of our nature. Our task is to ensure that it is accurate, that we can recognize ourselves in our own work of art. My experience leads me to believe that an accurate self-portrait will not leave us disappointed.

EXAMPLE:

Careless actions of a group of hikers allow their campfire embers to linger on. Sustained by a gentle breeze, they ignite the nearby dry grass and leaves. From there, the flames travel to shrubs and trees. They soon develop into a full-blown forest fire. The wind picks up and steers the blaze down the face of the mountain, bringing devastation to several small settlements that are located in the area.

Like the other residents of an affected village, Steven is trying to fathom the situation and figure out how to respond. The circumstances have provided him with an opportunity to have a whole range of experiences. He can experience himself as a victim of circumstances by angrily protesting against the disaster that has endangered his life. He can experience himself as a compassionate individual by comforting those who were badly affected by the fire, either by being physically hurt or by having their property destroyed. He can experience himself as a strong-willed, resourceful individual by leaping into action and leading the relief effort. He can have many other experiences as well, and combine them in myriad ways. It all depends on how he uses the present circumstances.

The Role of other People

The role of other people is indistinguishable from that of circumstances – they add to the richness of our palette and increase the detail of our self-portrait. Because people have feelings, values, and preferences and are able to communicate them to us, interacting with them has a definitive effect on our ability to express ourselves.

EXAMPLE:

Sally announces to her parents that her boyfriend of the past two years has proposed to her and that she has agreed to marry him. She knows that her parents don't approve of him, but she expects them to respect her independence and the ability to make her own decisions, including ones of this magnitude. Much to her surprise, both parents again express their dislike for her boyfriend and are vocally critical of her decision to make that mistake permanent.

Her parents' handling of the situation gives her an opportunity to have a whole range of experiences. She can experience herself as a victim of her parents' controlling behavior by going along with their preference while resenting it. She can experience herself as a considerate individual by trying to understand the source of her parents' views and the extent to which they were shaped by social conditioning and their own life experience. She can experience herself as a strong-willed, independent individual by willfully defying her parents' wishes. She can have many other experiences as well, and combine them in myriad ways. It all depends on how she responds to the feelings and behavior of the people whom she is interacting with.

Summary: Questions to Ask Myself

What am I trying to accomplish with the living of my life?

What kind of interplay do I see between external codes of conduct that I've embraced and the internal standard advocated by deliberate living?

How do I approach the people and circumstances that I encounter?

Criticism of the Underlying Life Philosophy

"When I recovered from my wounds they sent me home. Everything was the same and nothing was the same. My family, my friends, everybody was in slow motion, zombies in lock step, more dead than alive. There was nothing but people trying to impress their peers or attract the opposite sex. I couldn't stand it."

A Green Beret, Vietnam veteran

Several objections to this approach to living are sometimes raised at this point. Some of them stem from lack of familiarity with such an intensely purposeful way of life. Others are leveled from the perspective of well thought-out life paths that are different from the one proposed here in some crucial respect, and this difference is cause for alarm.

The purpose of this chapter is not to discredit the objections. I have come to realize that deliberate living is not for everyone. Considering how much I have benefited from it, this was not easy for me to grasp. Where criticisms involve erroneous assumptions of what deliberate living is about and how it works, I would like to clarify ideas so that readers can construct a better analysis of whether this approach to living has something worthwhile to offer them.

Intensity

The first objection highlights the intense nature of deliberate living: it simply takes too much time and effort to live life at this level of awareness, assign it this much purpose, and subject it to this amount of scrutiny.

This criticism stems from a fundamental misunderstanding of deliberate living. The perception being that it is a time-consuming activity that one would like to pursue, but just cannot find time for. As a result, it ends up being neglected in favor of more urgent pursuits.

In reality, deliberate living is not just a set of activities that is added to life as it is now, but one that transforms it by approaching all of the other activities in a new light. It does demand a considerable investment of time and effort, but not as a separate add-on to regular life. That add-on has to seep into everything else that we do, or it will be ineffective. It has a lot in common with the saying "I don't have enough time to be disorganized". The investment, sizeable as it is, pays off many times over.

To put matters in perspective, not wanting to incorporate the principles of deliberate living into our endeavors amounts to saying that we are too busy doing something to pay attention to what it is that we are doing, why we are doing it, or whether we approve of it being done.

This might sound like an unwarranted claim. Surely we can tell whether we like something or not without much effort? It seems obvious enough that this should be the case, but evidence suggests otherwise. There is a great deal of sadness, anger, and frustration that has found residence in our lives that can be eliminated by changing either our external circumstances or our attitudes toward them. Deliberate living assists with both.

The difficulty, though, is that it is next to impossible to anticipate the effects that such a purposeful approach to living is going to have without actually trying it out. I didn't look for it either. It was only some time after I had engaged in the process that I began to realize what my life had been like prior to that. As per the quote that introduces this chapter, it is a challenge of adding intensity to everyday existence without having to live through war to notice its absence.

I suspect that many people will experience difficulty seeing the present state of affairs for what it is until they find a way to step away from it. Until this is done, deliberate living will likely be perceived as a remedy for ills that don't exist and its potential will therefore remain untried and untapped.

Seriousness

A related objection questions not our ability to accommodate such a demanding change in our lives, but the desirability of doing so. Thoughts of frequent analyses of one's behavior give the matter a sense of heaviness that appears to be at odds with carefree, spontaneous living. Instead of enhancing it, it seems to take the fun out of life.

This impression assumes that deliberate living is about dispensing with fun in favor of more serious matters. In fact, deliberate living maximizes our engagement in life in every respect, including having fun. Spontaneity is surprisingly important to this process, as will be seen in part two of this book. I have found that deliberate living has really enhanced these aspects of my life – by clarifying what it is that I enjoy, helping me engage in it more fully and accompanying it with fewer regrets.

However, it is true that these benefits are arrived at by tackling life's big questions head on. Some people I have come across have no desire to do this. They prefer carefree existence that is not so burdened by responsibility. This is influenced by the challenges that one has had to face in life and has a lot to do with age. There comes a time in most people's lives when existential questions that were not important at all in their youth gradually come to the forefront. Deliberate living can wait until then.

Self-centeredness

It should be clear by now that the approach to living outlined in the previous chapter is self-centered. The focus is on the self and the self is treated as the highest authority in the decision-making process. Other people are reduced to a supporting role that facilitates the attainment of the primary goal, which is self-expression.

This raises serious alarm bells for many people. This is at least partly due to the attitude towards self-centeredness that is dominant in our society. It is perceived as a hurtful, destructive force that needs to be curtailed if our personal relationships and society at large are to function. This perception is supported by many examples of how indulging one's own needs and desires leads to marginalization and neglect of the needs and desires of others.

In response, consider the difference that is made by the level of awareness. At a low level of awareness, self-centered behavior can easily be counterproductive. Small children, for example, may have a hard time sharing, even though not doing so leaves them without playmates, and so is not in their best interest.

We can argue on the basis of this example that self-centeredness is a problem and needs to be overcome, but we can advance the same argument against lack of awareness as well. At a high level of awareness, self-centered behavior doesn't produce results that are harmful to the self. From my experience, neither does it produce results that are harmful to others.

Having said that, some people find it more natural to consider the needs and desires of others than to give such intense focus to their own. Some others find that a self-centered approach too easily devolves to a low level of awareness, where the behavior that they naturally engage in is to everyone's detriment. If this is the case, then it would be better to adopt an alternative approach, as described in the <u>Alternatives</u> section of the chapter <u>The Underlying Life Philosophy</u>.

Difficult Circumstances

Another objection that is sometimes raised is that this approach to living can be a real challenge to follow in situations that are difficult or painful. This is especially true if we choose to take responsibility for the circumstances in which we find ourselves, in addition to taking responsibility for how we respond to them.

For example, we may hold unconditional love towards all people as our highest ideal. Yet if we were to find ourselves in a traumatic situation, such as witnessing the murder of a loved one or being physically assaulted, it would be extremely difficult to react to it in a manner that is consistent with this ideal. A great deal of time would have to pass for such an approach to become a practical possibility.

It is important to realize that the goal of this book is not to present an approach to living that is easy to follow, but rather one that is worthwhile. It asks the question "Which approach to living brings about the most desirable results?" and then looks for ways in which it can be realized. The resulting insights can be difficult to implement at times, but if implemented, they should always be worth the effort.

We can take heart from examples of the few exceptional individuals whose lives leave no doubt that it is possible to conduct oneself according to one's highest ideals even in the most grueling of circumstances. The life of Mahatma Gandhi and his uncompromising commitment to non-violence is one well-known example. A less known, though by no means lesser, example is that of Maximilian Kolbe, a Polish Catholic priest who didn't step away from love and compassion even as he was being tortured in the Nazi concentration camp of Auschwitz, eventually volunteering to be killed in place of a man he hardly knew.

These are examples of deliberate living at the very height of its potential. They may appear to be hopelessly beyond our reach. They still look distant to me, too, but not as distant as they once did.

Summary: Questions to Ask Myself

What activities can I let go of to make space for deliberate living in my life?

Part 2:
How Is Deliberate Living Achieved?

The Placement of Responsibility

"To succeed, we must first believe that we can."
Michael Korda

Having made the foundational decision of what kind of relationship we wish to have with living our life, and having chosen a practical approach to realizing it, it is time to find ways in which this approach might be implemented.

The starting point on this journey is the question of responsibility. What is it that we are going to take responsibility for and how much responsibility are we going to accept? It might seem odd that this should even be a question. Given the wide range of attitudes that popular belief systems adopt towards the question of responsibility, however, it is one that needs to be dealt with before we can move on to more substantial matters.

Assuming Personal Responsibility

There are many ways in which the question of responsibility can be phrased. A form suitable for this discussion might be: *On whose authority are changes in my life made?*

It is a simple question. Most of us probably have ready answers. However, those answers are likely to differ from one person to the next. This variability is of interest because not all answers lend themselves to the pursuit of deliberate living equally well. Some present serious stumbling blocks.

As is evident from part one, deliberate living is inherently self-centered. An approach to life that emphasizes consciousness, thoughtfulness, and authenticity requires us to assume a great deal of personal responsibility for our conduct.

Unfortunately, it has become our culture to give away personal responsibility for many aspects of our lives. For good or ill, we have erected social structures in its place. We have become reliant on those structures to tell us how we should live our lives. As long as this is the case, we cannot progress on the route towards deliberate living because the decision of how to change our lives is not ours to make.

Examples abound. Probably the most widespread example of externalizing the decision-making responsibility concerns the judiciary. While we generally recognize that legality doesn't necessarily correspond to morality, the two concepts easily become blurred in daily decision-making. It is all too easy to think that the speed limit is a reliable driving guide irrespective of road conditions, or that not stopping at a stop sign is wrong even if the intersection is clearly deserted. It may be just as tempting to let legislation guide our professional conduct, as if rules and regulations can fill the void left by lack of trust and compassion.

The difficulty is more pronounced in the religious domain because the distinction between morality and adherence to religious rules is not easily appreciated. We can even shy away from taking responsibility for the shaping of our worldview by unquestioningly adopting the metaphysical assumptions that presently dominate the scientific establishment. This can be especially problematic if these assumptions contradict our personal experience.

Another way of looking at this is to observe that we are the only ones who suffer the consequences of every single decision that we make, regardless of whether we do so consciously or not. Therefore, we have a profound interest in taking responsibility for the making of those decisions.

The Scope of Responsibility

The decision to take personal responsibility for our conduct immediately raises the question of the scope of that responsibility. What are we taking responsibility for? How we act? What we say? What we think? How we think? What we feel? What we believe?

Do we take responsibility for these things in all circumstances, or just in some? Are we responsible for them when we are acting unconsciously, due to force of habit, intoxication, or grief? Do we take responsibility for them when we lack knowledge of cause and effect, lack familiarity with circumstances, or act on misleading clues given by other people? Do we take responsibility for the circumstances themselves?

If your children are as mad about Spiderman as mine are, you've probably heard the phrase "with great power comes great responsibility". A question that I find even more intriguing is whether the opposite is also true. Is it accurate to say that with great responsibility comes great power?

As should be clear from the previous section, if we accept no responsibility and completely defer to external authority, we have no power to make changes in our lives at all. That power rests exclusively with the external authority to which it has been deferred. Like an actor on a theatre stage, we help bring the play to life, but don't write the script.

Accepting responsibility changes that. If we decide that it is up to us to choose how to live our lives, then our role becomes one of an active participant at every level of the process. We get to select which insight from which source – external or internal – we will embrace as our own, and to what extent. The more facets of our lives we choose to approach in this manner, the greater our influence over them.

This tale comes with a word of caution. As has been noted by many influential people, power is a double-edged sword. The more power we have, the greater the potential for positive change, but also the greater the potential for disaster. It all hinges on our ability to use it wisely.

If we accept responsibility for our words and actions, then every word that we say and every action that we take that carry any significance need to be sanctioned by us before they are expressed. We can no longer rely on external authority – most commonly in the form of state or religious law – to justify our conduct. We also become responsible for being aware of our conduct and need to work to maintain this awareness in the face of habit, intoxication, and grief.

If we accept responsibility for our thoughts, then every thought we think that carries any significance needs to bear our stamp of approval, not only before it is transformed into words and deeds, but before it is even thought. We can no longer let our thoughts run loose as if they had a life of their own, outside of our control.

If we accept responsibility for our beliefs, then we must also accept responsibility for deciding the purpose of those beliefs. If our goal is the pursuit of truth, then we must be prepared to follow the evidence wherever it leads. If our goal is to empower ourselves to lead the best life possible, then we need to filter beliefs based on the consequences of their adoption, regardless of their truth standing.

If we accept responsibility for our emotions, then we become responsible for being aware of what we are feeling at any given moment. We also need to develop sufficient understanding of cause and effect to know which circumstances, and what interpretation of those circumstances, cause us to feel positive emotions. Then we need to use the appropriate interpretation whenever the opportunity presents itself.

If we accept responsibility for our circumstances, then we cannot perceive ourselves as their victim. We need to recognize our role as their willing co-creators. Alternatively, if our involvement is not a conscious one, we need to at least acknowledge their usefulness in what we have set out to do. Like the people from part one of the book – Steven facing a forest fire and Sally facing her disapproving parents – we need to utilize the circumstances that present themselves to create an experience that we genuinely desire.

A guideline can be derived from the above analysis – we shouldn't take on more responsibility than we can handle. If we lack the necessary skills to use responsibility in a particular domain in a constructive manner, we would probably be better off not accepting it in the first place.

If our goal is deliberate living, then another guideline presents itself – we should work to develop the capacity to use responsibility wisely. If accepting responsibility for our circumstances leaves us self-critical and paralyzed, for example, this is a sign that we need to cultivate the faculties that will enable us to use this responsibility constructively. As those faculties are developed, we will gradually be able to accept increased responsibility with positive outcomes. In turn, this will give us greater control over our lives, and greater capacity to effect the change that we wish to make.

How do we develop these faculties? What do they even look like?

In a single word, the characteristic that they all share is *attitude* – that of indomitable positivity and unbridled optimism. This attitude can take the form of different convictions. It might cause us to believe that the mastering of the relevant skills is well within our grasp. Alternatively, we might recognize them as more distant, but still ultimately attainable. We may even see them as beyond our reach, but thanks to our calm acceptance of this state of affairs, still find value in their pursuit.

At its core, adopting such a positive attitude amounts to nothing more than a decision to do so. As simple as this decision may be to make, it is by no means easy. Like other sizeable decisions, it depends on our ability to notice its absence, appreciate its benefits and summon the courage to put it into practice. Again like other decisions, it can be made considerably easier by familiarizing ourselves with insights and techniques described in the remainder of this book.[3]

---

[3] Martin Seligman's book *Learned Optimism: How to Change Your Mind and Your Life* contains practical guidelines for adopting a more positive attitude.

ALTERNATIVES:

The amount of responsibility that we accept will shape the nature of the approach to deliberate living that we choose to follow. It will also determine the portion of its full potential that becomes available to us. It is useful to keep that in mind if we shy away from some of the responsibilities at this stage. As our capacity for coping with responsibility grows, we may need to revisit the question so as to chart a course that has now become more appropriate.

Summary: Questions to Ask Myself

On whose authority are changes in my life made?

When taking responsibility for different aspects of my life:
Which aspects am I going to take responsibility for?
How much responsibility am I going to accept?

How do I develop the ability to accept more responsibility in a constructive manner?

Cultivating Awareness of Our Conduct

One of his students asked Buddha, "Are you the messiah?"
"No," answered Buddha.
"Then are you a healer?"
"No," Buddha replied.
"Then are you a teacher?" the student persisted.
"No, I am not a teacher."
"Then what are you?" asked the student, exasperated.
"I am awake," Buddha replied.

Once we have decided on which aspects of our existence we are prepared to accept responsibility for, we need to become thoroughly aware of them. For example, if we have decided to accept responsibility for our actions, whenever we commit a significant act, we need to be aware of doing so. If we have also chosen to accept responsibility for our thoughts, we need to be aware of every thought that exerts influence over us. Without awareness, we cannot even discern our involvement in our lives, much less evaluate or improve them.

There are several ways in which our awareness may be lacking, each one with its distinct causes. Together, they can conspire to rob us of experience, perceive our surroundings through a filter of value judgments without realizing that we are the source of those judgments, and engage in behavior that we feel is beyond our control.

The practice of mindfulness plays a central role in overcoming these difficulties. Mindfulness has its origin in Buddhism and Yoga, but is in no way constrained by their religious and cultural trappings. It simply amounts to concentrated awareness of the present moment, and the thoughts, words, actions, and feelings that are contained in it.[4]

Multitasking

When we undertake more than one activity at the same time, only one of these activities usually commands our attention. The others are done unconsciously for the most part, without our awareness of doing them.

EXAMPLE:

Since her retirement, Elizabeth has formed several new routines. One of them is drinking tea with her best friend every morning. They would get together on Elizabeth's patio, share in the tea and some biscuits, and chat about their plans for the day and many other subjects of mutual interest. They do the same today.

As she is listening to her friend, Elizabeth brings the cup up to her mouth, takes a sip, and then puts it back down. She does this several times, sometimes talking in-between the

---

[4] A worthwhile introduction to the practice of mindfulness is the book *The Miracle of Mindfulness* by Thich Nhat Hanh.

sips. Eventually, the cup is empty. The realization jolts her into awareness of the tea-drinking activity. She realizes that she cannot remember the taste of the tea from any sip after the first. She even has difficulty recalling the action of drinking it. The conversation was so enthralling that it had her complete attention. She engaged in the act of drinking the tea unconsciously.

The interesting feature of this process is that our experience depends on our awareness of the activity that generates that experience. If we lack awareness of the activity, we will forego the experience, and we will traverse our memory in vain searching for it.[5]

This might seem like a trivial objection to multitasking. After all, it's not as if we can eliminate it altogether. We receive sensory input all the time. Even if we could simultaneously pay attention to all of our senses, this would still leave us unable to do anything else. So why raise the objection?

The objection is raised, not because we engage in multitasking, but because we typically have very little control over it. When having tea with a friend, it makes sense that we should give the conversation our undivided attention. The significance of drinking tea pales in comparison. In this instance, drinking tea is a suitable background activity.

This in itself isn't a problem the first time it happens. However, as we participate in this activity and others like it, we gradually form a habit. The habit tells us that drinking tea is a suitable background activity, not just in a particular instance, but every time. It doesn't wait for us to decide wheth-

---

[5] I'm referring to ordinary attempts at retrieval. The experience can still be retrieved (relived) through hypnosis.

er drinking tea is worthy of our attention; it decides on our behalf that it is not, without so much as giving us a say in the matter.

As a result, we engage in routine activities without paying attention to them regardless of what is competing with them for our attention. Whether we are interacting with a friend, planning a future task, recalling a pleasant memory, or letting our minds wander aimlessly, the routine activity remains firmly in the background, safe from being experienced.

If certain activities are consistently not experienced due to our attention being focused away from them, we will be unable to evaluate the experience that they would ordinarily give rise to, and therefore unable to ascertain its desirability.

Furthermore, the manner in which routine activities are typically pursued is not conducive to their enjoyment. Because we have learned not to value them, we approach them with the goal of getting them out of the way as quickly as possible, or at least with little regard for how they could be made more enjoyable than they are now.

EXAMPLE:

Elizabeth has just returned from her afternoon walk. It's a hot day and she is sweaty, tired, and thirsty. She helps herself to a bottle of cold water from the fridge and starts gulping it down. The rushed drinking action helps quench her considerable thirst, but is itself stressful. Some of the water goes down the wrong tube and makes its way to her lungs. She stops drinking and starts coughing in an attempt to get it out.

After she has recovered, she decides to change her approach. She resumes drinking, but more slowly and mindfully, taking the time to appreciate each sip. She finds that, while taking longer, this manner of drinking is more effective at quenching her thirst. Not only that, but it makes the whole experience more enjoyable.

In essence, we are deciding that routine activities are not worth our while without even evaluating them. The decision to disregard them is therefore an uninformed one. It doesn't follow from a carefully thought out evaluation process, but from force of habit.

A way to break this habit is to form another habit, one whose task is to bring our attention to the present moment. We need to make a conscious effort to pay attention to what our senses are telling us. We also need to do this frequently enough to prevent unconscious routines from forming.

It must be stressed that routines are very useful. The goal is not to dispense with them, but to exercise control over what goes into them. If we were to examine our routines, we should not be surprised with what we find there. They should comprise activities that we have evaluated and intentionally relegated to the background.

It is also useful to keep in mind that our interests are not static – they change over time as we grow and mature. Activities that captivated us in the past might not do so in the future, and those that lurked in the background might later come to the fore. Background activities can reassert themselves intermittently, or gradually rise to dominance.

EXAMPLE:

While driving to work, Brad is normally absorbed in his own thoughts. The things that he hadn't finished the day before that would no doubt be waiting for him when he arrives;

the new tasks that are likely to come his way; the meetings and discussions that he needs to hold. He plays all of them out in his mind, anticipating how they might unfold.

Today, he decides to break from the routine. His driving takes him past a row of trees growing on either side of the road. He admires their substantial size and the canopy that their branches form over the road, and revels in the intermittent shadows that they cast across his path. Having emerged from them, he takes in the splendor of the clouds that he can see in the distance ahead of him. Some housing estates pass by on the left. He notices their spacious layout and appreciates the gracefulness of their design. The whole scenery comes to life, as if he's encountering it for the very first time.

EXAMPLE:

Having spent the first few years of his IT career focused on the problem of designing and developing fast and reliable computer applications, Dave begins to perceive the role that other people play in the process that goes beyond their technical contribution to the task at hand. He notices that they have preferences for different aspects of those challenges, even though they are competent enough to tackle them all. He also realizes that they handle the obstacles differently. Some become stressed by the looming deadlines and problems with their work while others handle them without a visible emotional reaction. He has seen this before, Dave realizes, but never taken more than momentary interest, disregarding it in favor of dealing with the technical challenges.

Now he finds it fascinating. It opens up a whole new world for him. Over a period of several years, he begins to pay more attention to the feelings of people who are impacted by his work than to the technical challenges that it entails. In fact, the extent to which they affect other people's emotions becomes the measure of the importance of those challenges.

Chattering

If we pay attention to our mind, we will notice that it is in the habit of chattering – generating running commentary on whatever we happen to be focusing on. We may be so used to this commentary that we don't even recognize it as commentary, but accept its content as an integral part of the person, object, or action that it refers to.

EXAMPLE:

Mary was standing by the ironing board, diligently ironing the clothes that her family was wearing last week. She glanced at the pile that she still had to go through. Its size exasperated her. The shirt that she was currently busy with had creases that resisted her repeated efforts at flattening. Their stubbornness infuriated her. Blocked steam outlets from her iron didn't help. As bad as that was, it was the thought that she would have to face the same wrinkled clothes week after week that really depressed her. She wished that she could afford to hire someone to do this work for her.

Perceiving our mind's commentary on the object of our attention as an integral part of the object itself amounts to relinquishing responsibility for that commentary. We cannot accept responsibility for what we are thinking if we don't realize that we are the source of those thoughts.

This perceptual error can be corrected by bringing our attention to the commentary that the mind is busy generating. The idea is to detach ourselves from the emotional imperatives that the thoughts give rise to. By declining to participate in the accompanying drama, we gain the ability to look behind the scenes to uncover the source of that drama. There we discover that it stems from our own thoughts. In other words, it is not a part of external reality.

Once the realization is made, other discoveries follow. We might come to understand how we have come to harbor the thoughts that we do, learn that we have the power to distance ourselves from them or replace them with other thoughts of our conscious choosing. A whole world of possibilities opens up.

EXAMPLE:

Having finished ironing her husband's shirt, Mary hangs it up and then reaches into the pile of un-ironed laundry for the next piece of clothing. She cannot help but notice the size of the pile. *I'll never get through this*, she thinks to herself. The thought brings on a tinge of desperation.

She catches herself in the act of entertaining that thought and immediately interrupts her routine. Why was she thinking that? The pile is indeed large, but there is no need to focus on its size and let that dominate her sentiments about the activity. She didn't like where the thought led and was determined to step away from its negative implications, choosing to concentrate on something positive and uplifting instead.

She notices her favorite blouse resting on one side of the pile. She pulls it out and lays it across the ironing board. She remembers the time when she bought it, how she gazed at it through the shop window mesmerized by its appearance and disheartened by its price until, quite spontaneously, she decided to make it a special occasion and treat herself to its stylish beauty. She lovingly runs her fingers across its folds. They feel as soft and opulent as when she first wore it. Then she follows her fingers with a hot iron, leaving flattened creases in its wake. The texture of the blouse feels warm and luxurious to the touch. It brings a smile of warm remembrance to her face. After intimately familiarizing herself with it once again, she carefully puts it away to continue with the next item from the pile.

Like the problem of multitasking from the previous section, the greatest difficulty with overcoming it is that we forget to bring our attention to the present moment. It helps to form a habit of paying attention to our thoughts. The more frequently this is done, the more easily we will remember to do it again, and the more informed we will be about our mind's exploits.

Automatically Responding to Circumstances

A similar habit can be found in the domain of words and actions. Sometimes we may feel compelled to act in a certain way by the circumstances that we find ourselves in. Our reaction may be conscious in that we are aware of what we are doing, but nevertheless feel powerless to change it. Alternatively, we may get so caught up in the drama that we lose sight of our role in it and perform it unconsciously.

EXAMPLE:

The Wednesday evening bridge game was the highlight of Michelle's week. She would get together with three friends after dinner, spend several hours catching up with the events in their lives, enjoy their company, and intermittently play cards. It was their scheduled fun time.

What made it more fun was that her friends were sure to bring some juicy story along with them that they could relive together. Be it a dimwitted work colleague, a short-tempered shop assistant, or that inconsiderate neighbor with the annoying poodle, there was always someone to deride or criticize. Michelle found herself unable to resist derision. She joined in the remarks with the skill of a seasoned professional.

Such behavior is made possible by failing to perceive a distinction between the circumstances that we face and our reaction to them. As a result, we allow circumstances to determine the nature of our response. Because we don't choose the response, we are unable to take responsibility for it.

In essence, whenever we use the circumstances that we are in rather than the consequences that we wish to produce as a justification for our conduct, we are relinquishing responsibility for it.

The problem is closely related to the chattering from the previous section. Similar mechanisms are at play. Because thoughts tend to become actions, allowing them to run without channeling them in a preferred direction is likely to cause our behavior to follow suit. Consequently, reining in the thoughts will give us greater control over our behavior.

In addition, the practice of mindfulness can be brought to bear directly on the behavior. If we detach ourselves from the emotional drama that we see in our circumstances, refraining from taking part, we gain the ability to observe and examine our actions. This allows us to realize that actions are something that we create and not merely experience. Once the realization is made, other discoveries can follow.

EXAMPLE:

Michelle's friend Susan was busy retelling a disturbing incident that took place at her work earlier in the week. It sounded like that nasty co-worker from the finance department had it in for her; even his tone of voice changed to something utterly despicable when he gave Susan his piece of mind. Michelle was used to hearing that tone of voice. It seemed that everyone who had something mean or unpleasant to say to Susan adopted it for the purpose of conveying the message. She wondered why they did that, since it only made them less likable and an obvious target of criticism.

Then it struck her: they didn't! It was a voice used by Susan to cast them in a bad light; it wasn't something they actually did. She realized that she had acquired the same tendency, albeit less pronounced, from associating with her friends. It was really a psychological defense mechanism, one intended to display them in a favorable light no matter what the circumstances, and so avoid facing up to the true nature of those circumstances and potential faults on their part.

Susan completed retelling the incident. Her friends gasped in response to the severe mistreatment that she had suffered at the hands of her co-worker. Michelle gasped as well, from the drama that filled the room that she now saw with a rare rush of clarity. Susan's story had been intentionally biased in her favor. She realized that all the stories told in their group were biased in the same way. Their goal wasn't to seek advice or constructive criticism, but simply to condemn all the people who were in any way unpleasant to them. Now that she saw the behavior for what it was, she couldn't help but wonder how she got caught up in it.

Experiencing Pain

Circumstances that we face sometimes give rise to an additional factor that thwarts our attempts at establishing control over our reaction. That factor is experiencing pain. The pain can be either physical or emotional in nature, though emotional pain is far more common in the modern world. Both kinds are very effective at eliminating our sense of perspective and thereby influencing our choice of response.

If we perceive ourselves to be injured, we will be motivated to protect ourselves from the injury. This will cause us to react defensively, perhaps even retaliate. Such a reaction is likely to be unconscious, especially if the hurt is severe. It will not be a carefully crafted response aimed at a particular desirable outcome, but thoughtless lashing out brought on by pain. It is about inflicting pain for the pain that has been caused, regardless of other consequences.

EXAMPLE:

With the youngest of her children finishing school and on his way to college, Claire was looking for a new project to keep herself busy. A local coffee shop that was for sale caught her attention. She knew the area. It was a decent neighborhood where most of the customers were regulars. It looked like something that two people would be able to handle quite comfortably. She spoke to a friend of hers, Denise, who was also looking for work and was delighted to discover that she shared her enthusiasm. They put their money together, took out a loan to make up the difference, and purchased the shop.

A few months into the venture, Denise started slacking off. She would come in late, leave early and not complete all of the tasks that she had taken on. Claire learned that she was having personal problems that prevented her from fulfilling her responsibilities in the shop. As much as she sympathized with her friend, she could only shoulder her share of the burden for so long before she also started buckling under the strain.

Soon thereafter, Denise declared that she wanted out of the venture with immediate effect. Claire was horrified. She had come to depend on her friend and couldn't bear the thought of working without her. The work that the two of them could complete comfortably was more than either one of them could bear on her own. Finding someone hardworking and trustworthy enough to replace Denise would take time. And then there were loan repayments to be made.

It was all just so overwhelming. Claire felt let down by her friend. As far as she was concerned, they had a contract in place, and Denise should honor it. As much as she sympathized with her for having personal problems, they were really not Claire's concern.

This is quite unlike a situation in which no injury is perceived. There, we feel free to consciously choose the most beneficial course of action. Having no need to protect ourselves from the intended abuse, we can examine the situation deeply to empathize with the other person, uncover his motivation for engaging in such destructive behavior, and help him heal.

Another way to look at the boundary between constructive and retributive responses is in terms of availability or freedom of choice. When no injury is sustained, we find ourselves at liberty to pursue any course of action we wish. Experiencing pain restricts our choices. The hurt compels us to react in certain ways, taking the matter beyond our control.

It might seem like a prudent course of action to avoid potentially painful situations. However, such situations carry within them the seeds of intense positive experience and tend to be opportunities for immense personal growth. Rather than avoid them, it makes more sense to me to look for ways to minimize or altogether eliminate the hurt that is normally associated with them. There are various ways in which this can be done. I have found the approach to living presented in this book fairly effective in this regard, as described in the section <u>Not Getting Hurt</u>.

When suffering does hold us in its grip, then the deliberate living imperative is to re-establish control over our reaction. In other words, our primary goal is to overcome the pain. We do this by seeking healing appropriate for the kind of pain that has been caused. Only once the healing has been effected and the choice of response is ours again are we in a position to respond to the circumstances that had brought on the pain; only then can we take responsibility for our own reaction.

EXAMPLE:

Claire's decision to hold Denise to their contract did the trick. Feeling guilty for abandoning her friend and not wanting to face legal action, Denise agreed to stay for another three months, as stipulated in the contract. However, her earlier pattern of not carrying her share of the workload continued.

Realizing that the ploy wasn't working after all, Claire decided to explore alternatives. It occurred to her that she had allowed herself to become much too dependent on Denise. If something were to happen to Denise, she would have been in serious trouble.

As she started considering other potential options, her spirits lifted. The quandary wasn't nearly as grave as she had come to believe. College holidays were approaching, which meant that her children would be able to help out at the shop. Her husband was too busy with his own work during the week, but he could lend a helping hand on weekends. She could think of several other friends and family members who might be able to help, and this was before even advertising for the position.

She was still clear that she couldn't keep the business going alone, but now she realized that the associate didn't have to be Denise. The change in perspective enabled her to approach her friend in a different light. She was able to let her go, to their mutual relief, confident that there were enough other people who cared about her well-being and that of the shop to see the venture through.

Summary: Questions to Ask Myself

Am I aware of the running commentary that my mind generates? Do I notice the judgments that it contains?

With respect to habitual behavior:
Which circumstances do I respond to habitually, without being aware of my actions?
What activities do I habitually engage in without paying attention to them?

With respect to experiencing pain:
How do I heal the pain caused by other people's conduct?
How do I avoid lashing out while I'm hurting?

Identifying the Consequences of Our Conduct

"The greatest obstacle to discovery is not ignorance — it is the illusion of knowledge."

Daniel Boorstin

Words that we utter, actions that we take, and, perhaps, thoughts that we think constitute our influence on the external world. The consequences of that influence are perceived both intuitively and through the physical senses. These perceptions influence our thoughts and feelings, which inform the next step of our behavior, setting in motion a repetition of the cycle.

There is a wealth of information here. All of it combines to create a richly colorful experience. It also presents an impossible challenge for our minds to analyze. If we are to successfully subject our experience to analysis, we have to reduce the amount of information that we are going to consider.

Consequences as Feelings

It makes sense to me to focus our analysis on the domain of emotions. These form the basis of our preferences, which in turn merge to form specific goals. It is thanks to emotions that we choose to act one way rather than another, or to act at all. When looking for justification for our actions, whatever we marshal in their support is itself rooted in experiencing positive emotions, even if this might not be obvious. Feelings are the only motivator and the only justifier that itself doesn't require further motivation and justification.

Even something as seemingly automatic as going to the toilet when the urge overcomes us is a matter of preference. A marathon runner, for example, may exercise a preference not to interrupt the running of the race in order to relieve himself.

A relatively simple, albeit costly, action of purchasing a new car is likely to affect our finances, our status, our outlook on life, our sense of self-worth, and many other things as well. All of these effects are the consequences of that action. Yet their effect is primarily felt by the emotional state that they provoke in us. If they fail to affect us emotionally, be it directly or indirectly, then it is worth questioning what it is that we stand to gain from analyzing them.

ALTERNATIVES:

Alternative approaches follow from choosing to focus on different consequences. Having said that, I can't think of any viable alternatives. We cannot go with pure reason because it embodies no preference. Working with a subset of consequences relevant to an external standard also falls short, for reasons outlined in the chapter <u>The Underlying Life Philosophy</u>. What this leaves us with is to select a subset of consequences to evaluate against an internal standard, but one that is not rooted in emotions. I don't see how such an approach can work without giving us a strong sense that something has gone awry.

A further deliberation that needs to be made is whose feelings we are going to consider. True to the self-centered nature of this approach to living, it is our own feelings that are placed under the spotlight. This is done because they are vital to formulating goals. We cannot tell whether a goal is worthwhile if we don't know how we feel about it. Because our feelings form the foundation of our goals, the consideration of our feelings is of central importance to deliberate living.

What is the role of other people's feelings, as well as the feelings of other creatures that we know or suspect are imbued with them? As described in the section <u>The Role of other People</u>, it makes sense to me that they should play the same role in decision-making as the circumstances in which we find ourselves. They do not help us formulate high-level goals. What they do help us with is to decide how best to pursue those goals.

If we take perhaps the most obvious general human goal – happiness – as an example, we can decide that this goal is worth pursuing purely on the basis of personal experience, without having to take other people's feelings into account. It is when we are faced with the prospect of realizing the goal that knowing the emotional states of other people in a variety of situations becomes indispensable to us. In other words, we don't need familiarity with other people's feelings to decide what goals to pursue, only how best to pursue them.

ALTERNATIVES:

When discussing the objection of self-centeredness in the chapter <u>Criticism of the Underlying Life Philosophy</u>, it was pointed out that, at a sufficiently high level of awareness, doing things for oneself yields very similar results to doing things for others. We can seek to do what is in our own best interests and notice that it also benefits others, or we can seek to do what is in the best interests of others and notice that it benefits us as well. They are just different filters through which we can interpret the same set of interactions. We can choose which approach to take based on what we find easier to work with, since the results that they produce are similar.

What Is the Self?

A discussion of self-centeredness naturally raises the question of what the *self* is. Within the context of this text, the self can be defined as whatever we perceive ourselves to be. This definition is exceedingly elusive, as the answer differs from one person to the next and for the same person at different times and in different situations.

There are many things that we can self-identify with. For example, we can see ourselves as our body when it is hungry or thirsty, reveling in sensual delights, or suffering from acute ailments. We can also see ourselves as our family during a festive gathering, while it is going through a financial crisis, or trying to come to terms with a loss of one of its members.

On a larger scale, we can see ourselves as our neighborhood or community when it is in need of new or upgraded infrastructure, as our company when it is developing a new product or service, our sports team when it is competing for a trophy, our culture when we interact with people from a different cultural background, our nation when it is under attack, our race when it attains exceptional achievements, our gender when we struggle to relate to members of the opposite sex, or our species when we wish to set ourselves apart from the multitude of life forms with whom we share this world.

Under exceptional circumstances, we can even identify with things that we otherwise clearly recognize as not being a part of us. A well-developed character in a novel can move us to tears, as can her convincing portrayal on a movie screen. Trials and tribulations of a character in a video game can likewise become terribly important. Even breaking into our house or trespassing on our property can feel like a personal violation.

More abstract concepts also lend themselves to this kind of use. We can self-identify with all living creatures and work for the benefit of life in all its guises. We can self-identify with our beliefs and feel personally attacked whenever they are criticized. If these stem from people we idealize, discovering flaws in them can lead to profound disillusionment. If we believe in a transcendent aspect of our being, we can self-identify with it to the limit of our understanding. We can even perceive ourselves to be an inseparable part of everything that exists, identifying with the universe and the worlds beyond.

As nebulous as this definition is, it is pertinent to the discussion because what we self-identify with influences how we conduct ourselves and changes in this perception give rise to changes in behavior. Even if we are clear at the intellectual level that our property is not who we are, for example, emotional attachment to it can nevertheless cause us to act as if it were an inseparable extension of ourselves.

EXAMPLE:

Jim's troops were on a reconnaissance mission outside of the friendly territory when they suddenly found themselves in an ambush. Bullets were zipping all around them. Several of the soldiers were shot before they even had a chance to respond. A few others barely managed to drop to the ground and fire at the unseen enemy before being blown apart by grenades.

Realizing the hopelessness of the situation, Jim made a quick decision to withdraw. Their only hope was to run for their lives. He shouted for everyone to retreat. He didn't know whether there was anyone left to hear the command. He was about to turn and run when he saw his close friend emerge from the low shrub to follow him. Barely did he get up when the bullets cut him down in his stride. He was wounded but still alive. His only hope was for Jim to carry him out of there. Jim knew that if he tried that, they would both be killed for sure. He turned and moved as fast as he could while keeping low to the ground.

His conscience screamed for him to turn back and rescue his wounded friend. This was not him. The fear for survival that drove his decision was not who he really was. He could easily rationalize the decision that he had made, but his emotions were telling him otherwise, as irrational as that may be. They left no doubt that the person he really was would look out for the well-being of his friends no matter the circumstances, even as he ignored the dictate of his conscience in his frantic attempt to escape.

The question of what kind of self we should identify with can be answered by recognizing that, as critical as this decision is, it is still nothing more than a decision. It is not a straightforward decision in the sense that we can simply decide to self-identify with all of life, or to stop self-identifying with the body, and from that moment on, the desired change in behavior follows. Nonetheless, once we make the decision to change what we self-identify with, there are ways in which it can be gradually put into practice. This is explored in more detail in the first example from the section <u>Purposefully Adopting Beliefs</u>.

ALTERNATIVES:

At a low level of awareness, the choice of what to self-identify with can have a drastic effect on our behavior. If we self-identify with our body, for example, we may be tempted to look at other people, animals, plants, and minerals as beings and things that can help satisfy our physical needs and desires, but that have little value beyond that.

At a high level of awareness, this difference largely disappears. If we pay attention to our feelings, we will notice the value of taking heed of the feelings of other people and the beauty of treating other creatures and things with care and reverence. Our behavior will become more considerate regardless of whether we choose to enlarge our self-definition to encompass that which we are considerate towards.

Distinguishing between Thoughts and Feelings

Identifying the consequences of our actions in terms of emotions that they produce might seem simple, and it often is. Provided that we have sufficient awareness of our emotions in the present moment, we will invariably feel the effects and recognize what it is that we are feeling. However, there is one significant complication. In addition to recognizing our feelings, we will also recognize our thoughts. This is not ordinarily a problem except that some of these thoughts have a tendency to masquerade as feelings.

How do we distinguish between the two? A critical point of difference is that, unlike feelings, thoughts are mental constructs. They are a result of mental processes that we engage in. This is obvious when these processes are conscious and not so obvious when we engage in them unconsciously. If anything, this makes awareness of our thoughts and feelings all the more important.

This distinction has several implications. The first one is that thoughts cannot arise from situations with which we have no prior acquaintance. Because thoughts are a product of mental processes, and these processes require data on which to operate, absence of this data prevents them from taking place. Of course, we are generating the necessary data by the virtue of having the new experience. However, the delay between thoughts and feelings is noticeable.

EXAMPLE:

Nick had just passed his driver's test. With the license under his belt, he couldn't wait to get his hands on his dad's car to take it for a spin without the hindering company of one of the adults. That afternoon he did just that. He left the house for a joyride around the neighborhood without a destination in mind.

It started to rain. Lacking the experience of a seasoned driver, Nick reveled in the excitement of slippery conditions, until he approached a turn too fast and watched helplessly as his car spun out of control. It moved in dreamy slow motion, with the driver too terrified to do anything but look on as it did a pirouette across the road. A few long moments later, it came to a standstill against the curb.

His mind blank, he just sat in the car, frantically trying to make sense of what had just happened. It took a few seconds for his mind to assimilate the brand new experience. What was he thinking? His dad will kill him when he finds out! He better hope that the car is not damaged too badly. At least he didn't remember hitting anything other than the curb. He stepped outside to assess the damage.

We also need to keep in mind that the notion of a brand new situation is more complex than may appear at first. The experience of the ravages of war, for example, is not new if we have spent time living in a war-torn region or country. However, it is also not new if we have seen it dramatized in a movie, reported on television news, read about in newspaper, heard about from a refugee, or learned about in any other way. None of these methods of acquiring information can substitute for the genuine experience, but they nevertheless provide us with data which our minds can analyze. Depending on how comprehensive this data set is, the thoughts that result from it when we are having the actual experience may avoid detection and pass themselves off as genuine feelings.

Another implication is that strong thoughts can be triggered by experiences that don't trigger strong emotions. This tends to occur in circumstances that are ordinary for the most part, except for some detail that stands out for us due to our preconceived ideas about it.

EXAMPLE:

Harry has been raised in a home where competition and drive for success were high on the family's priority list. As immigrants in what they saw as a land of opportunity, his parents took whatever work they could, and worked as long and as hard as they could, all in an effort to create a brighter, more prosperous future for themselves and their children. Having largely succeeded at it, they made sure to instill the same values in their children.

A side-effect of their accomplishment was that they had little patience with people who failed where they had succeeded. Harry internalized this attitude during his upbringing. The way he saw it, people who haven't created a level of affluence similar to that of his parents were simply failures who haven't tried hard enough.

He remembered the first time he came across a street dweller. His father had taken him to town and they were walking down one of the main streets. On the side of the street he spotted a man dressed in rags. His face was gaunt and dirty. Harry was disgusted by his appearance. The revulsion was so strong that he moved to the other side of his dad and hurried along in an effort to get away from the man as quickly as he could.

Resolving Apparent Contradictions

Why does the distinction between thoughts and feelings matter? After all, it's not as if we can switch our minds off and operate on feelings alone. Nor would we necessarily want to do this, even if we could, as it would leave us with a one-dimensional view of our experience. We are better off supplementing the feelings that we have in response to a situation with mental analysis of that situation.

The problem that we have, however, is that these two sources of information don't always complement each other; sometimes they contradict. Instead of joining forces to add color to our experience, they can work against each other to make it opaque. This can happen if our thoughts are not rooted in our experience.

The extent to which our thoughts conflict with our feelings depends on the extent to which we have internalized other people's views. This can occur at any stage of our lives, but is most prominent during childhood. Because these views tend to deal with matters on which we have no personal experience, we are not likely to notice that they originate from other people once we internalize them. It is precisely when we do experience circumstances related to them that we begin to question the accuracy of these internalized views.

EXAMPLE:

Harry met Byron at the local school that they both attended. They soon became best friends. Byron was a great guy to hang out with, simple and sincere. Perhaps too simple, in fact. Harry noticed that his friend always brought homemade sandwiches instead of buying food from the school tuck shop. His clothes and classroom accessories were also unsophisticated, old and well used. His family must have been poor.

Using his own family history as a reference point, Harry started offering what he thought was good advice on how Byron's family could improve their lot in life. He was confident that, with the right attitude, they could emulate his parents' success. He was startled to discover that Byron was being raised by his mother; his father had disappeared from their lives when he was small. He also had a younger brother whose childhood has been dogged with medical problems. Harry couldn't help but wonder whether his life would have turned out much better had the circumstances been similar.

Learning about Byron's family background left him utterly confused. He could see the considerable difficulties that they faced. He felt for their hardship and wished that he could alleviate it. Yet, at the same time, they were failures by the only yardstick he had ever used, the kind of people that he normally wouldn't even consider associating with.

Situations that confuse us in this manner don't arise from conflicting emotions. The conflict is between feelings and thoughts masquerading as feelings.

Overcoming False Internalized Beliefs

False beliefs can be overcome with sufficient exposure to contradictory personal experience. The process is by no means easy – strongly engrained beliefs can be particularly difficult to overcome – but this typically has more to do with strength and courage than the ability to distinguish between personal experience and internalized beliefs.

In some instances, however, personal experience never materializes. Sometimes the very presence of a false internalized belief precludes the likelihood of a contradictory personal experience. This is because we tend to reason our way to action. Reasoning is mental analysis of the relevant data, which in this case has been adopted from other people. Analyzing this data will steer us in the direction of the adopted conclusion, which will prevent us from acting in a manner that contradicts it.

EXAMPLE:

Harry was still finding his feet at his new school. His old friends were no longer with him. He still occasionally saw them on the weekends, but school days were lonely. As much as he hated being thrown in a class full of strangers, he knew that he was there to stay; the only option left to him was to get to know them and make new friends.

Byron caught his eye early on. A capable student, he was well liked by the class. He was easy to get on with, sincere and undemanding. It was his academic success coupled with his tendency to accept people for who they were that attracted others and put them at ease. Harry was also drawn to it, until he uncovered the underlying reason.

Byron came from a poor family. His usage of worn and basic accessories was not an attempt to make others comfortable; it was all he had to work with. As much as this made him easy to be around in the school setting, it would also have made him an embarrassment in Harry's home and in his old circle of friends. Byron wasn't someone he could seriously associate with.

If we are to challenge such beliefs, we need to generate our own data for our mind to analyze. This will enable us to reach conclusions that are different from the ones that we have adopted, and more in line with our feelings. Since it is thinking about the course of action to take that prevents us from generating this data, we need to act before we think. We need to act on impulse, before our minds reason us out of it.

EXAMPLE:

Harry, Byron, and two of Byron's friends were having lunch at the school grounds. The classes were finished for the day. Afternoons were usually filled with extracurricular activities – such as sports and cultural pursuits – or simply doing homework.

Byron's mother arrived to fetch him from school. In her usual style, she invited his friends to come with him as well. She didn't live far from the school and it wasn't much of an inconvenience for other parents to fetch their kids from her house or for her to take them back to school later on. Since Harry was having lunch with them, the invitation automatically applied to him as well.

He was reluctant to go, but couldn't think of a good excuse. He didn't have any school commitments to attend to, just some homework to do. Other kids were urging him to join them. On the spur of the moment, he gave in to their persistent cajoling and decided to come with them to Byron's house.

He immediately started having second thoughts. The car that Byron's mother used felt a bit dodgy; reliability didn't seem to be its strong point. The neighborhood that they lived in wasn't the best and their house was modest. He was definitely going to ask her to take him back to school rather than have his parents fetch him from there.

As he settled into his new surroundings, however, he noticed that it had a different ambiance to it. It somehow felt open and comfortable to be in. He noticed that, instead of talking down to him, Byron's mother treated him as an equal. There also seemed to be very few household items that she prized and considered to be more valuable than the children themselves. He felt more at peace and accepted here than in his own home.

As he was being taken back to the school in time for his parents to fetch him, he was struggling to make sense of the experience. He still had reservations about being friends with Byron and especially introducing him to his parents, but the ways of his parents no longer appeared as unassailably correct as they once did.

Summary: Questions to Ask Myself

Where do I place the boundary between myself and other(s) in different situations?

Which elements of my experience am I going to subject to analysis?

Which internalized beliefs conflict with my experience?

Which internalized beliefs prevent me from acquiring relevant personal experience?

Evaluating the Consequences of Our Conduct

"There is more learning in the question itself than the answer."
Andrew Weremy

Having decided on the aspect of our experience that is best suited to evaluation, the next step is to go ahead and analyze it. If we have settled on emotions, this is not as straightforward as it may appear. As was pointed out in the previous chapter, distinguishing this aspect of our experience from others can be a challenging task. In less emotive, everyday situations, we might face an unexpected challenge of not having a perceptible emotional reaction for us to evaluate. Perhaps the most formidable challenge is posed by the conflicting nature of emotions. All of these factors combine to make evaluation of our behavior a demanding process, one that warrants considerable attention.

There are various guidelines that can be offered to assist with the process. The purpose of this chapter is not so much to offer an exhaustive list of guidelines, but to examine their nature and see how they work, so that we may develop the tools with which to formulate new guidelines as the need arises.

The Value of Questions

Before we delve into the evaluation, it may be useful to examine the quote that introduces this chapter. It is one of the many sayings that emphasize the importance of asking the right questions as opposed to having the right answers. Because this sentiment has been shared by many influential people, it may be tempting to accept it uncritically, without appreciating the wisdom that it contains. Why are questions more valuable than answers?

To appreciate the difference in the context of deliberate living, it is necessary to understand that deliberate living is a journey. It is a process of continuous refinement, an ongoing change towards greater clarity and greater authenticity. It is not a fixed point. The dynamic nature of this process mimics the nature of questions more closely than that of answers. Put simply, questions are more valuable than answers because answers are static while questions are dynamic.

There can be no doubt that having the right answers is extremely useful. We cannot live authentically if we lack intimate familiarity with our likes and dislikes. If we know, for example, that making a positive difference in the lives of other people fills us with unbridled joy, then we have a good idea of what goals to pursue in situations where this course of action is a practical possibility.

The shortcoming of answers is not that they are not useful, but that their scope is severely limited. If we examine answers more closely, we see that they accurately describe who we were at the time when we acquired them. It is merely an assumption that they accurately describe who we are now. This assumption is only valid if no significant growth has taken place between the two points in time.

If important matters in life were static, it wouldn't really matter how we acquired answers to them; we could hang on to those answers for the remainder of our lives. Because they are dynamic, however, the process that we follow to acquire those answers becomes critical; we have to traverse it more than once.

Questions are more valuable than answers because they enable us to derive answers as the need arises. They extend a single set of answers valid at a point in time into a continuum that ideally mimics our evolving understanding of ourselves. The ability to do so is an indispensable tool. This is what makes deliberate living possible.

EXAMPLE:

Brad spends a lot of time commuting daily. He drives his own car to and from work. A lot of this commuting takes place in congested traffic. He finds that his emotions run high when he gets stuck in a long line of slow-moving cars. He has little patience with other people's driving errors and next to no tolerance for their trying to cut in front of him.

Realizing the undesirable nature of this approach, he asks himself what changes he should make so that his behavior is more in line with what he would like it to be. Thinking about a near-incident of road rage when he came close to having a tussle with another driver, he realizes that he should stop with the outward display of his frustration, since it further provoked the other driver who, like him, was reaching the limits of his fortitude. He makes a concerted attempt to stop with his practice of hooting, flashing lights, shouting, and pounding at the steering wheel.

As he gets into the habit of toning down his outward display, he realizes that all he has accomplished is to release the same negative emotions through a different outlet. Where he used to get visibly angry, he now passes sarcastic remarks to himself. Sometimes he puts on a smile, but it is just a cover up for how he truly feels.

Realizing that his new behavior is almost as undesirable as the old, he has another go at looking for ways to improve it. He decides that the endless critical remarks about the events on the road have to go. He is able to gradually cut back on the commentary, finding that he has developed a habit of keeping quiet about the events that used to provoke violent outbursts.

It doesn't take him long to discover that his control of the outward display of his emotions has done nothing to improve the emotions themselves. His mind still latches on to driving that differs from his and passes ready judgment. This still causes him to feel angry and frustrated. It's just no longer audible or visible in his conduct. Understanding the danger of bottling up emotions, he looks for ways to improve his handling of the situation even further.

It occurs to him that there are many beautiful things that catch his attention while he is driving under less strenuous circumstances. Sometimes he passes picturesque scenery, be it rows of trees or elaborate houses and estates. Sometimes clouds form stunning displays in the sky above. Lovely music or engaging commentary and dialogue can sometimes be heard on the radio. He realizes that he can focus on these things even when grappling with rush-hour traffic.

As his focus shifts away from the slow driving pace and the misdemeanor of other drivers, the judgments disperse and the strong emotions that used to ferment in him are also left behind. He becomes progressively calmer and more contented. He still occasionally catches himself mentally criticizing displays of inconsiderate driving, but it is an exception rather than the rule. When he does get sidetracked with negative commentary, he is able to shift his focus away from it and leave the incident behind.

With his improved emotional state, he finds that he now has the capacity to return some of his attention to the previously stressful conditions on the road without automatically reacting to them in a negative way. This gives him an opportunity to look behind the inconsiderate, sometimes downright rude behavior of other drivers in an effort to make sense of it.

He begins to notice parents with small children in the car. He doesn't have any children, but some of his friends and members of the extended family do. He has been around them enough to know that he doesn't want them anywhere near him while he is trying to contend with rush-hour traffic. He starts to sympathize with the stressed out looks on the faces of parents who are in this unfortunate situation.

As he spends more time dwelling on the subject, he makes many other observations as well. Drivers that slow down before every intersection, even though they have the right of way, used to annoy him. Now he realizes that they are probably unfamiliar with their surroundings and are looking for street names and other landmarks to help them find their way. Broken down cars that block traffic used to be a major irritation. Now he feels for the people who are stuck without transportation of their own and who, on top of being late and becoming dependent on other people to take them places, also have to make arrangements to have their car towed away and repaired.

Over a period of several years, thanks to concerted effort at introspection and continuous refinement of his approach, Brad's demeanor changes to what he genuinely wants it to be.

Analyzing Straightforwardly Emotional Situations

From the perspective of evaluating decisions, this is the simplest kind of situation that we can face. Because evaluation is centered on emotions that we feel, it doesn't get any easier than dealing with situations where our actions elicit a strong and unambiguous emotional reaction. Not much of a guideline for evaluating decisions made in this kind of situation is needed. Asking a simple question like *"Do I like the way this makes me feel?"* is typically sufficient.

EXAMPLE:

Helen is seated on a spectator chair of the execution chamber. She is about to witness a particularly gruesome event, yet one that she has been looking forward to for several years. Ever since the murder of her daughter, she has invested all her energy in seeing the murderer brought to justice. In her mind, this meant execution. Now that she was moments away from achieving that goal, she felt a grim sense of satisfaction.

The criminal was brought in and strapped to the electric chair. He didn't look like the cold-blooded killer that she remembered. She heard a cry from the other side of the room. It must have come from someone in his family. They were also present at the execution. She wondered what it was like for them. It must have been traumatic, but then so was her daughter's murder.

The high-voltage current coursed through the convict's body. It lifted and strained in response. Helen was distressed to discover that she could feel the current-induced pain. His family's wails intensified. They could feel it too. She quickly slipped away from the scene of the execution. She thought she would enjoy seeing her work come to fruition. Now she was distraught that she derived no pleasure from the event and didn't have the stomach to face his family in the aftermath.

The reality of the situation dawned on her that evening in the privacy of her own home. The hole that her daughter had left in her life loomed as large as ever. Seeing the murderer executed for his crime didn't help patch it at all. In fact, it made matters worse, for now she had no one to vent her fury on, nowhere to deflect the emptiness that she felt. His disappearance only aggravated her sense of loss.

The voice of conscience comes to the fore in straightforwardly emotional situations. It provides a corrective influence – it manifests most forcefully when our conduct falls far short of the ideal. This makes it a valuable addition to the examination of our feelings that can be found in the wake of our actions.

Analyzing Ambiguously Emotional Situations

Not all emotionally charged situations that we can encounter are so unequivocal in the feelings that they stir. Sometimes the response is experienced on several levels and it tugs and pulls us in multiple directions. When this occurs, it helps us to find ways to simplify the situation by cutting away the ambiguity.

A way to do this is to identify specific motives that we are intimately familiar with and that we have come to trust to guide our decisions. Then we determine what decisions these motives would give rise to. We can think of them as model solutions to the conundrums posed by specific situations. Lastly, we compare these solutions with the decisions that we have actually made. The actual decisions are deemed desirable to the extent that they match the model solutions.

EXAMPLE:

Judy was sitting in the kitchen anxiously smoking a cigarette. It was her routine for calming her nerves. Right now they were positively shot. After their latest fall out, her husband had gone to the pub to regain his own sense of composure, but not before leaving her with a black eye. It was the latest in the series of physical abuses that she had endured at his hands during their turbulent marriage.

Having calmed down, she did her best to analyze the situation sensibly. She was reminded of their marriage vows, when they promised to love and honor each other for the remainder of their lives. It was an ideal that they both believed in, and still do, even if they were having a hard time living up to it as of late. She wondered how she would react if her actions were motivated purely by that ideal. What would she do if her actions were rooted in love?

She understood that, if she truly loved herself, she would put a stop to the abuse. She also understood that, if she truly loved her husband, she would not seek to return the abuse in kind. She realized that her actions had been motivated by a variety of factors, and that this had allowed her to put up with abuse from her husband that she would not have tolerated had she proceeded from her highest ideal.

In addition to looking for known trustworthy motives in search of model solutions, we can also look for motives that we can rely on to lead us astray. The process is similar to the above, except that the model solution in this case tells us what decisions to avoid.

EXAMPLE:

As she is pondering the situation and wondering what to do, Judy is gripped by fear. It is all good and well deciding to stop tolerating the abuse, but how exactly will she put a stop to it? It has been going on for several years. She cannot expect her husband to suddenly change and stop taking his anger and frustration out on her physically. She would have to leave, at least for a while, until he came to his senses and came to respect the boundaries. She wasn't sure that this would ever happen. But would he let her leave? What if he came after her? She would have to disappear secretly and not leave a trace for him to follow. If she succeeded, what would she do? She doesn't have work, not even a formal qualification to her name. She would have to take whatever jobs she could find just to support herself. It all felt so overwhelming.

She recognizes that this is fear talking. She has come to distrust fear due to the paralyzing effect that it had on her. She understood the value of being careful and anticipating things not going according to plan, but if she gave in to her fears and behaved accordingly, she would be permanently stuck in the familiar cycle of abuse, unable to break free for fear of what that might entail. She decides to step away from this course of inaction.

Analyzing Unemotional Situations

Unlike the problem from the previous section where we had more information to deal with than we could handle, the problem with situations discussed in this section is that they don't give us enough information to work with. When this happens, we need to find a way to boost the signal, so to speak.

This can be done by asking questions whose purpose is to stimulate an emotional response that is otherwise lacking. The idea behind these questions is to exaggerate the consequences to such an extent that we cannot help but respond to them.

EXAMPLE:

Terence was busy filling in his tax return form. The activity always brought on a pang of regret. He disliked being reminded of the money that he was donating to the government. It was necessary for society to work, he knew, but the thought of earning money that he couldn't use nevertheless left him dejected.

His eyes fell on the section of the form that dealt with traveling expenses. He received a tax rebate proportional to the mileage that he covered during the year. He just had to pretend that all his driving was business-related and increase the figure accordingly, and watch some of the tax money come back to him. He may as well; he would be surprised if other people didn't do the same.

The thought was quickly followed by another: Was this really him? Even if other people did the same, he couldn't use their behavior to justify his own. What if his actions were to become public knowledge? What if everyone followed his example? Would he still do what he was thinking of doing? He didn't like the implications, the exposure of such actions to public scrutiny, or the statement that they made about what kind of person he was. The previously inconsequential decision started to matter to him a great deal.

Evaluating Predictable Consequences

As we gain proficiency with asking and answering questions like these, the consequences that they give rise to become more predictable. We become able to safely anticipate their occurrence ahead of time. This makes it possible to evaluate the consequences of those decisions before even making them.

A difficulty that we may still face is that we forget to perform the evaluation. Some circumstances can be grueling or downright overwhelming. The sensibility to perform the needed analysis can be hard to come by in such situations. What we need to do in these cases is distance ourselves from the present challenges so that we can bring the full power of our faculties to bear on the situation.

EXAMPLE:

Anne is jogging up the hill. Her tempo is brisk but measured. This is her third Iron Man competition. She needs to keep up her pace if she is to beat her previous time while leaving enough energy in reserve to last the duration of the challenge. She knows what result she wants and what she has to do to accomplish it, but her body is screaming for her to stop or at least slow down to a comfortable walk. The longer the challenge continues, the louder her body becomes and the more persuasive its demands.

To silence her body, Anne knows that she has to shift her perspective past the present arduous circumstances to what they will be after the decision is made and its consequences have come to pass. She knows what will happen if she gives up. She has done it before in different competitions as well as during training. What she needs to do now is project those consequences to the present situation to help her decide whether they are worth the physical relief that accompanies them.

Alternatively, she can shift her perspective to the consequences of her decision to persevere with her commitment to the contest. She has triumphed in enough prior competitions and training to be familiar with the sweet taste of success. Now she needs to project those consequences to the present situation to help her decide whether they are worth the pain that she is busy enduring.

Dealing with Conflicting Feelings

Apart from the challenge of identifying the feelings that a decision has given rise to, the evaluation process can also stumble because those feelings contradict one another. Emotions don't always supply us with a neat picture of reality, where we simply pursue what we like and avoid what we don't like. Sometimes they conflict, requiring us to choose what we value the most and trade one preference for another.

There are two general ways in which different parts of the message communicated via our feelings can be in conflict. The first one occurs when we receive conflicting messages by similar means, but at different points in time. A common example of this is the consumption of sweets, chocolates, cakes, and other foods rich in sugar. We absolutely adore the taste, only to be faced with possible weight gain, toothaches, and visits to the dentist later on.

Whether the good outweighs the bad depends on the circumstances – how much we like the good and dislike the bad, and how frequently and for how long each occurs. If we are unable to neutralize the negative effects of such decisions, a guideline that can be offered is to steer away from mixed blessings and instead pursue decisions whose outcomes are strictly desirable, if such a choice is available.

The second form of conflict results from consequences being simultaneously experienced in multiple ways. We may approve of them on one level and at the same time detest what we are seeing on another. One such example is enjoying the taste of meat that has been deftly prepared and deliciously seasoned, yet loathing the health and ecological implications as well as the cruel treatment that the animal may have endured.

As before, no reliable guideline can be offered for resolving these kinds of conflicts. I'm not aware of a way to do this besides comparing the intensity of each experience to decide which is more profound, and thereby which sensation comes closer to speaking the truth about us.

The Lure of Rationalization

Perhaps the most cunning pitfall that we can encounter when evaluating the consequences of our actions is to engage in their rationalization – post-hoc justification of the decisions that have already been made. The danger might not be obvious, so it is worth spelling it out in some detail.

Honest evaluation of consequences runs the risk of discovering that our actions have been detrimental. We may have failed to reach our goals or caused ourselves harm, either directly or by hurting those around us. This is a decidedly unpleasant situation to face up to, even if we understand the long-term benefits of doing so. A seemingly preferable approach is to deny its reality and look for ways to justify our actions. In other words, engage in their rationalization.

The similarity between the two approaches resides in rationalization giving the appearance of what evaluation of consequences seeks to accomplish – understanding of the good and bad sides of the aftermath of our actions so that we can gradually eliminate actions that lead to undesirable consequences and engage solely in positive ones. It looks this way because, after rationalization has been completed, we think we know why we have performed a particular action and feel fully justified in our conduct.

The difference in results, however, is staggering. While truthful evaluation of consequences facilitates our growth, rationalization assures us that no growth is necessary, and that our current approach is quite appropriate, regardless of what it may be. It doesn't amount to greater awareness or understanding of the decision-making process, but only to an appearance of that. We can even make decisions completely unconsciously, without so much as mastering the first steps of the process outlined in this book, and still succeed at rationalizing them. Similarly, we need not understand why a decision was made or agree with its outcomes in order to rationalize it and thereby provide some justification, however misleading.

EXAMPLE:

The introspective thoughts that held Terence back from fudging the figures on his tax return form soon gave way to a different way of looking at the situation. Relinquishing some of his money for the common good was necessary for the society to function, but was this the way to do it? The government was rife with corruption. How did he know that his money would find its way to the intended benefactors of their social programs? Not that he agreed with all of their policies anyway. Why was he financing them then?

The more he thought about it, the less reason he saw for handing over the money that the government expected from him and the more justified he felt in adjusting the figures to his benefit. In the process, he lost sight of the original motivation for doing so – the desire to keep as much of the money as he could for his own use.

The two approaches are relatively easy to tell apart. They ask different questions. Evaluation of consequences follows from their identification and attempts to determine how desirable they are. It reaches its conclusion on the basis of the analysis that it performs. Rationalization, on the other hand, assumes that the consequences are desirable and looks for reasons why. In other words, it starts with the conclusion and searches for the most plausible line of reasoning to get there.

Generally speaking, whenever we find ourselves searching for justification for a decision that we've already made, we are engaging in rationalization.

Summary: Questions to Ask Myself

When evaluating decisions:
Do I like the way it makes me feel?
What would I do if motivated by love (or some other positive motivation)?
What would I do if motivated by fear (or some other negative motivation)?
Is this who I am?
Would I do the same if my decision were made public?
Would I do the same if other people followed suit?
How will I feel about the decision after its consequences have come to pass?

Have I made the decision on the basis of evaluation, or have I simply assumed that the decision is appropriate and then tried to justify it?

Expanding Our Knowledge Base

"I have learned silence from the talkative, toleration from the intolerant, and kindness from the unkind; yet, strange, I am ungrateful to those teachers."

Kahlil Gibran

As we master the ability to evaluate the consequences of our conduct, we become able to tell which results are desirable to us and which ones we would rather avoid. We also learn which actions can be relied upon to produce them. All of these insights emerge from analysis of personal experience. This is the most direct, and so the most reliable and profound form of knowledge that we can have.

It is also severely limited in its scope. There are far more possibilities available in life than what we can directly experience. Many of them we wouldn't even want to experience, regardless of whether we had the opportunity. For these reasons, we need ways to decide which goals are worth our while and which ones are not, without first having to reach them in order to experience and evaluate their consequences. Similarly, we need ways of identifying the actions that will bring about those consequences without having to engage in them first.

These additional insights can be acquired in several ways. Some of them are rooted in observation of the external world. Others create a world within our imagination. Unlike observation of our experience, these methods are less eager to reveal their secrets to us and only do so indirectly. This makes them less reliable than analysis of personal experience. It is useful to keep this in mind should the two come into conflict. The role of indirect methods is to supplement personal experience with information that would otherwise be lost to us. They should not be used to invalidate it.

Given the richness of the external world and the breadth of the creative potential of our imagination, it should not be surprising that the diversity of impressions that can be gleaned from them is immense. Situations present themselves that reveal remarkable and atrocious goals in plain sight. Others trigger unexpected associations within us that turn out to be equally revealing. All of them offer priceless insights into the kind of lives that we want to lead.

What follows are examples from the non-experiential sources that I rely on, to illustrate the wisdom that they contain.

From Theory

This is perhaps the most obvious external source of insight – information conveyed by other people specifically for the purpose of personal growth. It is most frequently presented in written form, especially in books and articles. This is where its reach is the widest. However, video recordings have also become popular in recent decades, and direct contact with spiritual teachers is still sought by the more committed of us.

Perhaps the greatest value of these insights is that they can help unlock the growth that we have already achieved. They point out what we already know but haven't formulated into a nugget of wisdom or paid attention to before. Because we approach the teachings with the expectation of learning something from them, the words resonate with us as soon as we come across them. It is at this point that we recognize the wisdom that they contain. We can immediately relate to it because it is already validated by our past experience. All that was lacking was the final recognition.

EXAMPLE:

Of the people that Jeremy interacted with, there were a few that tried his patience. Their behavior was positively inapt – they were overly critical, inconsiderate of other people's feelings, demanding, and so on. He found them particularly difficult to handle when he had to deal with them on regular basis. Occasionally, it provoked an angry, frustrated response.

Upon reading the quote at the beginning of this chapter, the reality of the situation suddenly struck him – he had been learning valuable lessons from these people while simultaneously resenting having to deal with them at all. The clarity of the observation astonished him. It accurately described his reaction, yet stated it in such a way that it became obvious to him that he could have chosen a much more constructive response.

An interesting feature of spiritual teachings is that they may not carry the same meaning for us as they do for the person who uttered them, nor does their meaning necessarily get preserved as we learn and grow. There is no requirement for the message to remain static, or to accurately reflect the intended meaning of its originator. All that matters is that it speaks to us and helps us achieve growth that we would not have accomplished so readily in its absence.

Another benefit of spiritual teachings is that they can open our eyes to vistas that we may not have conceived of before. This is not easy to do because, in this instance, we don't yet have the life experience with which to relate to what they have to tell us. This makes it all too easy to simply label them as wrong and dismiss them. The challenge then becomes one of probing beneath the surface implausibility to see whether we can make sense of it, or even to try it out to see whether the resulting experience supports the spirit in which it was offered.

EXAMPLE:

Melissa had made a concerted effort to study the Bible and implement Jesus' teachings in her life. She saw great value in many of them. However, some of them presented her with considerable difficulties. His instruction to love one's enemies was particularly problematic. It wasn't ambiguous, which left her very little room to maneuver. She couldn't think of any plausible way to interpret it but literally. He didn't ask for tolerance or courtesy towards one's enemies, but for genuine concern for their wellbeing.

Not being able to make sense of it, she decided to try it out to see how well it might work. There were a few people with whom she was on very bad terms. Instead of continuing with the usual hostility, she decided to change her approach in line with Jesus' instruction.

She soon discovered that she couldn't love these people without understanding them, and she couldn't understand them without getting to know them. What she learned about them drastically changed her perception. She realized that they were people like her, with their own substantial problems. They either didn't appreciate where she was coming from, or didn't know how to deal with it. Understanding them made it very difficult for her to continue with the resentment.

Letting go of her hostility towards them provided another revelation. She was better off not harboring ill feelings towards them, even as their antagonistic behavior continued. Releasing the grudge ended their control over her. Instead of her response being dictated by their actions, she was now free to decide what she wanted it to be.

She was astounded to discover that loving one's enemies wasn't about self-sacrifice in the hope of some distant reward, but about acting in one's own immediate best interest.

From Observing Plants

Thanks to the astounding diversity of life that our planet harbors, there is a tremendous amount that we can learn by simply observing it. Hardly a moment goes by without us being exposed to some living creature as it goes about its daily business. The greatest challenge that this form of learning poses to us is to remember to take notice of it.

Even when we narrow our focus specifically to plants, the multiplicity of behavior that we are left with remains immense. Some plants enjoy a symbiotic relationship with certain other plants and animals; some others rely on thorns and toxins to keep intruders at bay. In pursuit of sunlight, some plants rely on growing to heights unattainable by their competitors; some others depend on their hardiness to withstand shortage of nutrients. Some plants spread and prosper by making themselves attractive to animals and humans; some others achieve the same through sheer tenacity.

It might not be obvious that plants have anything to teach us at all. Indeed, their capacity for expression is so different from ours that it might be tempting to disregard them completely and focus our efforts on acquiring spiritual insights from sources that closely resemble us. This approach is needlessly self-limiting. It is precisely because of this difference that plants are able to impart insights that we cannot easily acquire elsewhere.

It is not necessary to achieve accurate in-depth understanding of the plants' behavior in order to derive insights from it. As with spiritual teachings from the previous section, it is not about the world of plants as it is in itself, but about the associations that it triggers within us. Even if our observation of plants causes us to draw wrong conclusions about them, these mistaken inferences can still be of value to us if they lead us to make beneficial changes in our own lives.

EXAMPLE:

Having recently taken up gardening, Sandra made a point of spending some time in her garden every weekend. She had a bench erected by the house, at the entrance to the garden. She would sit on it and gaze at the greenery that was serenely growing all around her.

It always amazed her how the plants could lead such peaceful, carefree existence. It wasn't quite like that, she knew – they competed with each other for resources, albeit on a different time scale – but that knowledge was lost in the tranquility of the moment.

She closed her eyes to feel the gentle breeze on her skin. It soothed her to be in an environment that was so undemanding. It presented a stark contrast to her busy schedule. It required considerable effort on her part to take time out from all the activities to spend quiet time in the garden. Yet, whenever she did this, she was grateful for the convalescing effect that it had on her.

EXAMPLE:

As her eyes were taking in the beauty of the garden, Sandra focused on the flowers that many of the plants were adorned with this time of year. Not just the plants that she cultivated strictly for their appearance, but even some of the vegetables and the apple tree that was growing in the distant corner of the garden. Many bees were milling about them, happy to help themselves to the pollen that they supplied.

She compared the approach that the plants had chosen to follow – bringing forth the best of themselves in the hope of attracting the services of the insects that they depended upon – with a different approach that she frequently encountered in the human world – using force and coercion to accomplish the same. She realized that she, too, relied on the latter even in the presence of easily available alternatives. Disliking its effect, she wondered what it would take to let go of it in favor of the former.

From Observing Animals

Like plants, animals present us with their own unique perspective on life. It is not as alien to us as that of plants, so it is easier to relate to. Nevertheless, it is still sufficiently different to furnish us with some insights that we would struggle to attain elsewhere.

The animal world is likewise bountiful in its multiplicity. From herbivores to predators, from solitary hunters to insect colonies and gigantic herds, from burrowers to creatures of the sky, it is teeming with lessons for us to learn. There is no need to seek out the rare and the outlandish. Animals that we have become accustomed to and with whom we share our lives can teach us just as much.

EXAMPLE:

Eric's dog was his pride and joy. It was large and dangerous-looking, and did a good job of keeping an eye out on the property. Yet, for all its size and mean appearance, it was also very good with children. Some of the children from the neighborhood would occasionally visit and play with the dog. They would run around, kick the ball shouting and laughing and the dog would happily join in the fun.

Watching this, it occurred to Eric that his dog either didn't experience or was unaffected by mood swings that characterized the behavior of all the people he knew. Whenever he came home, the dog would happily wag its tail. Whenever a small child pulled on its fur, it would patiently tolerate it or, if it became too painful, move away. Eric realized that his own behavior fell far short of this ideal.

EXAMPLE:

Janet is busy watching a nature documentary on her TV. It features a pride of lions and their hunting habits. She sees a group of six lionesses stalking a herd of zebras. They set up an ambush – three of the older, stronger and slower lionesses take up position in the low brush downwind from the herd, while the other three move to the opposite side. The younger lionesses give chase, steering the herd in the direction of their hidden partners. One of the zebras is unfortunate enough to head straight for a hidden lioness. She tries to get out of the way at the last moment, but it is too late. With a practiced leap, the lioness latches onto the zebra's back and brings it down to the ground. The others are upon it within seconds. The zebra desperately tries to get away, but it is powerless against the combined might of six lionesses. After suffocating it with a stranglehold on the windpipe, they proceed to gorge on its innards.

Watching this, Janet is reminded of the food that she eats, where it came from and how it got there. There is striking similarity between the two. If anything, the lionesses' approach is the more humane. She now needs to decide whether she will allow the display that she has just seen on TV to describe her as well, or whether she is going to make a different choice.

From Observing Children

Children present us with an interesting paradox. On the one hand, because they have not been exposed to social norms to nearly the same extent as us, their behavior reflects human nature more closely in this particular respect. It is still influenced by popular beliefs of the society they live in — something as seemingly harmless as learning a language can be quite effective in this regard — but those beliefs haven't been internalized to nearly the same extent.

On the other hand, children have a particularly poor understanding of cause and effect. Their actions frequently produce consequences that are not to their liking. It is this disconnect between goals and behavior that leads me to conclude that, despite lack of socialization, their conduct doesn't convey human nature with a high degree of accuracy.

Still, thanks to their unique approach to life, observing them can help us arrive at some valuable insights about ourselves and the kind of behavior that we would do well to engage in or steer away from. This partly derives from the position of authority that we normally assume over them and the unbalanced relationship that this gives rise to.

EXAMPLE:

Drawn by the sounds of frustration coming from his son's room, Warren crept up to it and peered inside through the open door. He saw his son struggling with the toy car that was recently given to him as a gift. Then he angrily threw it on the floor, accompanied with some colorful language.

Hearing his son cursing at the toy jolted Warren from his passive, even amused observation of his son's demeanor. Where did his son learn those words? What kind of crowd did he hang out with at school? Then he remembered his wife's remark that he sometimes slipped into similar behavior when he was angry or frustrated. His son probably learned this behavior in his own home.

Warren realized that he was actually witnessing his own conduct reflected in his son's. It was like a theatre re-enactment of his life, with his son faithfully playing the lead role. Watching the display had an entirely different effect on him than when he was caught up in the midst of it. He didn't like what he saw. It just looked so childish. Instead of scolding his son for acting like that, he decided that he needed to set a better example for him.

EXAMPLE:

Cathy's daughter is a joy to behold. With eager curiosity and an innocent smile, she brings out the best in everyone who takes the time to play with her. She needs a bit of time to lose her shyness in front of strangers, but it's not long before she welcomes them into her play circle.

Cathy likes watching her daughter play. It is the difference between their approaches that captivates her. Cathy has a hard time trusting people. She struggles to let go of her suspicions and fears of being let down and hurt. Watching the carefree way in which her daughter interacts with other children and adults, she can't help but wonder whether this lack of trust is inhibiting her relationships, and whether placing fewer demands and expectations on them would have a liberating effect on everyone involved.

From Observing Adults

This is the most straightforward observation that we can engage in because we can relate to other adults from our society more easily than to any other beings mentioned in this chapter. We generally share the same assumptions about reality, which inform our interaction with it. We also have similar capabilities. These factors make the conclusions that we draw from observing other adults more directly applicable to our lives when we find ourselves in similar situations.

The downside of the increased similarity is that the range of behavior that we are likely to observe among other adults is comparatively limited. This is why it is beneficial to observe other beings as well, even if we may have a harder time drawing useful conclusions from them.

EXAMPLE:

Sonja was always at a loss for what to do in the presence of strangers. Be it in a doctor's waiting room or in a sparsely populated elevator, she would get flustered whenever her eyes met those of another person. She felt that she should say something to alleviate the awkwardness, but didn't know what. Other people seemed to be equally at a loss for a practical etiquette.

One day, as her eyes met those of an elderly man who was traveling in the lift with her, his face broke into a warm and gentle smile. There was nothing forced about it. He seemed to be genuinely contented with her company. She found herself disarmed by his relaxed demeanor. There was nothing that needed to be said; things were all right just the way they were. She was so spellbound by the sheer magnetism of his approach that she decided to adopt it for all future encounters with strangers.

EXAMPLE:

As far back as she could remember, Jennifer has wanted to be a celebrity. It didn't matter too much to her in what field – an actress, a musician, a sports star – as long as she got noticed. She watched on TV and read in magazines about how fabulously wealthy celebrities were and how they turned heads wherever they went. She longed to be like them.

As she got older, she also noticed what looked like the dark side of fame – lack of privacy and dependence on recognition of the fans for a sense of value. As much as she wanted to be noticed, she didn't want paparazzi to follow her every move. She most definitely didn't want her every misdemeanor to make newspaper headlines. As much as her body tingled at the thought of having fans that faithfully attended her exhibitions, she dreaded being judged by them should her performance not meet their expectations. This way of life had captivated her interest since she was small, yet now she found herself wondering whether it was worth the hefty price tag that it carried.

Adults have another advantage over other beings in that they are much better able to communicate their thoughts and feelings to us; we are not restricted to what we can observe. This communication is limited in its completeness and accuracy, but is nevertheless a useful addition to what information we can glean from observation of their behavior.

From Observing People from other Cultures

By *other cultures*, I mean radically different ways of relating to the world around us. This can entail holding fundamentally different assumptions about the nature of reality, since these support the structure of our worldview and govern our behavior. It usually entails valuing different things. It necessitates a wide chasm in lifestyle.

Strictly speaking, it is not necessary to travel far and wide to find people who function so differently from us. Thanks to the ease with which global traveling is accomplished nowadays, people from other cultures can often be found in the nearby vicinity. However, the very act of mixing helps to bring the cultures closer together. This is why greater variety can be found between cultures that have had minimal mutual interaction.

I have derived tremendous benefit from learning about indigenous cultures from various parts of the world. Their perspectives are so different that they have helped me become aware of many of the assumptions of the modern society that I have unconsciously internalized, and demonstrated ways of being that I hadn't considered before.

These people are not easy to observe. They prefer a life of isolation from the modern society. Contact that does take place is solitary and sporadic. Nevertheless, we can learn a lot about them from reading the many books that have been written as well as from watching documentaries.

Again, it is not necessary that we have a sound grasp of the beliefs and lifestyles of people from other cultures in order to derive value from them. Even if we completely misunderstand how they perceive and interact with the world around them, and in our misunderstanding stumble upon a way of living that is superior to our own, we would have gained something.

EXAMPLE:

While I don't entirely agree with the quote below, I think that it provides a useful contrast to the ways of the modern Western society:

> Words like *durable*, *guaranteed*, and *built to last* came to mind, words that had been etched into my mind by years of conditioning. I thought about the meaning of *construction* to the Shuar. It meant building a house that was intended to last only a few years; after that the house would be allowed to dissolve back into the Earth and a new one would be constructed somewhere else. It meant erecting a small dam for catching fish, which would be torn down before sunset. It meant a hammock made from vines, a blowgun of chonta wood and beeswax, and a dugout canoe. The concept of constructing something 'durable' was foreign to the Shuar, and to all tribal people. You did not want a thing to last; you wanted it to serve a specific, short-term purpose and then return to nature. How different their dream from the one I had been taught!
>
> I realized that our entire economy revolves around what we think of as 'heavy' industry and 'durable' goods, and that this is completely contrary to the natural world and those that live close to it. In nature, and among traditional societies, nothing is durable; everything is in flux. While our historians consider a bronze arrowhead to be superior to a wooden one, Núnkui and Pachamama would not agree; the wooden one is superior because it is less durable. The same

could be said for pottery, and for everything else that we make, shape, or mold.[6]

EXAMPLE:

I think that this quote describes a worthwhile dimension that, unfortunately, is largely absent from our existence – from the judiciary and often from personal relationships as well:

> It is said that in the Babemba tribe of South Africa, when a person acts irresponsibly or unjustly, he is placed in the centre of the village, alone and unfettered.
>
> All work ceases, and every man, woman, and child in the village gathers in a large circle around the accused individual. Then each person in the tribe speaks to the accused, one at a time, about all the good things the person in the centre of the circle has done in his lifetime. Every incident, every experience that can be recalled with any detail and accuracy is recounted. All his positive attributes, good deeds, strengths and kindnesses are recited carefully and at length.
>
> The tribal ceremony often lasts several days. At the end, the tribal circle is broken, a joyous celebration takes place, and the person is symbolically and literally welcomed back into the tribe.[7]

---

[6] Taken from John Perkins' book *The World Is As You Dream It: Shamanic Teachings from the Amazon and Andes.*

[7] Taken from Alice Walker's book *Sent by Earth.*

From Imagination

All of the methods of extending our knowledge base that we have discussed thus far are limited in what they can accomplish by the availability of personal experience. Without experience, we cannot relate to what we are reading or observing, cannot evaluate it to reach conclusions about it, and cannot productively incorporate it into our lives.

Imagination surpasses these limitations. It enables us to go beyond our direct experience in the pursuit of insight. It does this by recognizing the similarities between situations that we have lived through and those that we are trying to evaluate, and taking elements of our experience from the former to shed light on the latter. It is still dependent on the availability of personal experience – we cannot effectively imagine the possibilities in a situation for which we completely lack a frame of reference – but it can make the little experience that we do have go a long way.

EXAMPLE:

Melissa opened the kitchen tap in a hopeful attempt to wash her hands. Her hopes were quickly dashed. It was already night time, and they'd had no water for most of the day. It was frustrating. She has come to rely on running water as a basic necessity in life that one shouldn't have to go without.

She remembered that, as she was walking through the neighborhood earlier that day, she saw water running down the street. She didn't make much of it at the time, wondering whether someone was just being careless with their washing of the car or watering of the garden. Now she realized that it must have been a burst pipe that needed fixing. It was probably the municipal workers who shut down the water supply while they were busy with the repairs. It was infuriating nonetheless.

As irritated as she was, she paused to consider what the whole incident looked like from their perspective. They've spent most of the day digging up and replacing damaged water pipes. It was cold and dark now and they were still at it. She doubted that they would rather continue with their work than spend time with their families in the comfort of their own homes. She also didn't think that they were being paid particularly well for the work that they did. Even though she had never been in a similar situation, imagining what it must be like was sufficient to convince her that she wouldn't want to either.

The drawback of using imagination to help us evaluate situations that reside outside the realm of our direct experience is that the conclusions that we reach might not be accurate. How reliable they are depends on how closely the situations that we have experienced mimic the one that we are trying to examine.

EXAMPLE:

Like many other residents of the small industrial town, Shaun has spent his whole working life as an employee in the local steel factory. It was hard work with little hope of improvement, but one that put food on their table at the end of the day. He frequently interacted with the foreman, whose lot was slightly better in terms of pay and hazards at work. It was a position he hoped to fulfill some day.

Occasionally, he would catch a glimpse of people who were in charge of the place. Not just the people running the local plant, but those they reported to. At least that's who Shaun thought they were. He would see their shiny cars parked outside the administrative building. He could tell from their suits that money came easily to them, and from their demeanor towards the factory manager that they wielded a great deal of power.

He wondered what his life would be like if he were in their place. All the things he could do! All the respect he would command! Practically all of the hardships that he had to contend with daily would be a thing of the past. Never having been wealthy, he couldn't imagine the challenges that this would present, but he had a keen sense of how his life would benefit from such a change in fortune.

Another feature of imagination is that it relies on the same brain circuitry that our physical senses utilize. If we are trying to visualize something, how well we can do that depends on what visual input we are already busy processing. Even the simultaneous functioning of other senses can interfere with the process. It is useful to be aware of these difficulties so that we can have some idea of the reliability of the product of our imagination, as well as learn to utilize it under optimal conditions.

EXAMPLE:

While waiting at a red traffic light, John noticed a beggar standing by the side of the road. Her thin frame suggested that she hadn't had much to eat lately. He'd been hungry enough times to know what it felt like. However, on this particular occasion, he had just eaten a good lunch. The feeling of fullness made it difficult for him to recall those times of hunger in a way that reproduced the emotions associated with them. As a result, he couldn't properly relate to the beggar's perceived situation, even though he could discern it intellectually.

From Inspiration

By inspiration, I mean a sudden flash of insight that is not a direct product of our reasoning about a subject. In other words, it is not just a matter of drawing conclusions from data that we are busy analyzing, but makes an unwarranted leap beyond that data, if it is about the data at all.

Flashes of insight are not consigned to specific locations and times, so it might seem odd listing them as one of the sources that we can intentionally tap. While inspiration doesn't keep time and place, there are ways in which the frequency of its visitations can be increased. They essentially amount to placing ourselves in a receptive state of mind – through meditation or other such technique[8] – and thereby allowing it to come forth. The more relaxed and open our state of being, the more easily insights are able to enter our conscious minds.

---

[8] Strangely enough, the clearest exposition of these techniques that I have come across was in the last chapter of Casey Blood's book *Science, Sense & Soul: The Mystical-Physical Nature of Human Existence*. I say strangely because the book is not strictly about mysticism, but attempts to reconcile it with quantum physics and neuroscience.

EXAMPLE:

Alec has been a frequent gym visitor for the past few months, experimenting with all of the available exercise machines and weights. The rowing machine has become his favorite. He has found that he doesn't have to concentrate on what he is doing, but simply sit back and relax into the repetitive rowing motion. This allows him to close his eyes and get lost in the rhythm of the movement. It also helps him to work agitation out of his system.

Initially, he simply appreciated the beauty of it. While his body was preoccupied with the physical task at hand, his mind would soon wonder off to various matters that have engaged his attention during the day. It would replay them, analyze them, and use them to create new imaginary scenarios. Alec would become lost in his mind's meanderings, except for occasionally glancing at the screen to check whether he was done rowing for the day.

While in this state of mind, he found that he was able to withhold attention from other people whom he was sharing the gym with, as well as to let the music fade into the background. He also stopped checking the screen to see whether he was done, and instead paid attention to his body and mind to decide when to stop rowing.

Some sessions later, as his mind was busy casting one of his unfriendly work colleagues into an imaginary role of a villain, it occurred to Alec that he didn't have to go through with this and let his mind roam wherever it wanted. He could interrupt it and give it an opportunity to focus on something else, something that he found more enjoyable to replay, or saw more value in being analyzed.

With time, he noticed that, while his mind wasn't preoccupied with following a specific train of thought, it was unusually receptive to brave new ideas. They popped in unexpectedly and gave him new insights into problems that he'd been struggling with, or took him in completely new directions. His mind would latch onto these thoughts and start analyzing them with unusual lucidity. However, this would prevent brand new insights from emerging until he had brought the mind back to an unfocused state.

He found that he could facilitate his mind blanking out by focusing on the rhythmic rowing motion, or on the breathing that accompanied it. He could also allow beautiful music to stir up his emotions and thereby foster creativity. As he increased the frequency and duration of the blank mental state, the magnitude and quality of inspiration that he received during these sessions increased accordingly.

It might be tempting to think of the information received in this manner as revelations. I hesitate to use the term because it gives the appearance of divine instructions that leave no room for interpretation or disagreement. The insights that we acquire in this manner are still in need of our interpretation and approval before we can make constructive use of them. If doing so presents us with difficulties, then we should discard the insights that have caught our attention instead of insisting that we put them into practice due to their perceived privileged status.

The Prudence of Discernment

So far in this chapter, the assumption has been that the knowledge that we acquire from external sources can be put to use in our own lives. As long as we can clearly identify what it is, translate it into our own capabilities and put it into practice in similar circumstances, the results should follow.

This is not quite true. Only some of the knowledge that we acquire in this manner lends itself to such use. The benefits of other knowledge can remain forever beyond our reach, no matter how faithfully we might replicate the conditions within which we have observed it. The challenge to distinguish between the two is one of discernment.

The difference between the two categories of knowledge lies in the source of the effect. Some actions that we engage in lead directly to the consequences that we desire. As long as we master the art of generating the causes, their effects will follow. This is the case with the examples presented thus far in this chapter.

In other cases, the link between cause and effect is indirect – it proceeds via at least one other person. Because other people can also choose how to react to circumstances that they face, the choice of response is not assured. We can influence it by using our behavior to change their circumstances, but we cannot force the response that we want. That decision remains with them.

If we wish to pursue goals of this nature, we should keep in mind that we are not in control of whether we achieve them or not. Our efforts can increase the likelihood of success, but they cannot guarantee it.

EXAMPLE:

After graduating at the top of his class, Dave started working for the Information Technology Department of one of the leading banks. It didn't take him long to get to grips with its systems. Talented and ambitious, he set his sights on progressing to the position of the team leader, which he would then use as a springboard to further career progress and recognition.

To his frustration, the managers who were responsible for promotions in the team didn't see things the same way. They saw maturity and inter-personal skills as essential ingredients of any position of leadership. Dave had neither. What he had was unrivalled technical brilliance. As far as he was concerned, the people in the position of leadership should simply be the ones who excelled at the core skills that were needed in their team. In this case, it was designing and developing quality software applications. That's all there was to it. While he received informal recognition for his contribution in this area, the formal recognition of promotion to the team leader position remained beyond his reach.

Summary: Questions to Ask Myself

What insights have I gained from reading or listening to material aimed at fostering personal growth?

What insights have I gained from observing my surroundings?

What insights have I gained from learning about radically different ways of living and perceiving the world, such as those from other cultures?

How can I use imagination to extend my life experience to new situations?

How do I foster inspiration?

Which of my goals are under my control and which can only be reached if other people act in certain ways?

Tying Knowledge to Circumstances

"Anyone who has never made a mistake has never tried anything new."

Albert Einstein

Just as we need ways to decide which goals are worth our while before engaging in their pursuit, we also need ways to discern which actions will help us realize those goals without first having to take them. Some of these insights can be gleaned from observation of the external world, as described in the previous chapter.

This is a domain of functionality. Having identified the consequences that we find desirable, we now need to identify the behavior that gives rise to them. The amount of detail related to this subject is immense. If we consider human life in all its richness, each general goal can occur in countless situations, requiring a multitude of different approaches to realize it. If we wish to experience ourselves as competent individuals by mastering a difficult task, for example, the approach that we take can differ radically depending on which task we set out to master. This is why it helps to make peace with the fact that lack of knowledge will occasionally thwart our efforts, no matter how well intentioned they may be.

Because knowledge of causes is far more specific than the effects that they generate, it cannot be divorced from the knowledge of circumstances in which they can be applied. Adding this third dimension is necessary if knowledge of cause and effect is to have practical value. It also enables us to traverse the dependency tree in both directions – given a set of circumstances, we can decide how to act to bring about desired goals, and given desired goals, we can decide what circumstances to seek out to enable appropriate actions.

Knowledge of Circumstantial Potential

Having a firm grasp of the possibilities that exist in a particular situation is the key to applying the knowledge that was discussed in the previous chapter. The guideline is remarkably simple. We begin by noticing what is lacking in a situation. Then we provide it. The example below shows us that the act of provision gives us the experience of that which we provided.

EXAMPLE:

While sitting in his car at a busy intersection, John's attention moved to a lone figure that approached his car window. It was an elderly woman. Her skin was wrinkled, her face was dirty, her hair was disheveled and her clothes were old and torn. There was no doubt in his mind that she was struggling to get by and that her livelihood was entirely dependent on the generosity of others. There was hope in her eyes, though he could tell that she expected to be dismissed – the treatment that beggars usually received.

Seeing the difficulty of her circumstances, he reached for the money that he had in the car and gave some of it to her. It wasn't much at all, but he could tell from the excited expression on her face and the words of gratitude that it meant the world to her. She was holding material abundance in her hand. By giving it to her, he got to share in her experience.

It was only later when he analyzed the encounter that he grasped its significance. By giving her the money, he was effectively making the statement that he had so much that he could afford to give some of it away. It didn't matter how rich or poor he was relative to his peers or other members of his social circle, he was able to experience abundance by the simple act of helping to fill the material insufficiency that had dominated the woman's experience up until then.

As the example demonstrates, we don't need extraordinary circumstances to have an extraordinary experience. What we need is extraordinary awareness of whatever circumstances we happen to be in. This is sufficient to fill our lives with remarkable experiences, even if there is nothing remarkable about the situations from which they arise.

We should also be careful not to isolate the events that have granted us exquisite experiences and in so doing overlook all of the events in between. In reality, noteworthy opportunities present themselves all the time. Be it in the form of dishes that need washing or a cat looking for a rub, all of them allow some delightful aspect of our nature to come forth and assume an experiential form. It is purely a question of which of these circumstances we choose to utilize to the height of their potential.

This is not to denigrate astonishing experiences that occasionally take place. Infrequently, we get to touch another person in a profound way, or beneficially influence scores of people. These events certainly stand apart. However, if we succeed at unleashing the potential of even the most ordinary conditions, all of them get to add beauty to our lives.

Changing Circumstances

Growing familiar with the possibilities embodied in each set of circumstances allows us to string them together – identify situations that can be fruitfully sought given the present possibilities, and that enable their most beneficial expression. This effectively expands our options from a narrow set that is available in any specific situation. It is useful to keep this in mind if the choices that are immediately available don't appear to be all that appealing.

EXAMPLE:

Claire opened her fridge to examine its contents. It was brimming with all kinds of food. She came across an unusually good sale during her recent shopping expedition. Doing her best to make the most of the rare discounts, she bought much more food than she normally did, as well as some varieties that she didn't usually eat. Now it was sitting in her fridge, waiting to be consumed.

Looking at the wealth of food, she grew increasingly anxious over it going bad before she was able to eat it. She could vacuum pack some of it and store it in the freezer for long-keeping, yet there wasn't much space available there either. She could also compost the food that went bad. Neither possibility looked particularly appealing to her. Instead, she decided to share all of the extra food with other people, and in so doing give herself the experience of abundance.

Empathy

Grasping the possibilities in a situation that doesn't involve other people is generally straightforward. It can also be fairly uncomplicated in the case of extreme circumstances – such as life-threatening danger and intense grief – where recognizing and appreciating other people's feelings and desires doesn't present much of a challenge. However, many of the situations that we come across are not so clear-cut. Understanding what the other people are going through, and in doing so what opportunities the situation presents us with, can be a difficult task.

That task can be eased by developing three skills. The first of these is empathy – the ability to share in the experience of other people. Of course, we cannot directly share in their experience. Even if we could, this wouldn't necessarily be desirable. If someone is suffering, our goal is not to suffer with them, but to ensure that neither of us suffers. It is about understanding suffering, not partaking in it.

The way to do this is to visualize ourselves to be in the same situation and pay attention to the resulting experience. It won't be nearly as intense as if we were to actually be in that situation, but hopefully it will be sufficient to give us an inkling of what the other person is going through.

For the simulation to be effective, however, it is not sufficient that the circumstances be the same; the way we interpret them must also be similar. Otherwise we might picture ourselves in the other person's shoes and wonder what all the fuss is about. If we are naturally optimistic and the other person is a pessimist, for example, we might not see a problem where the other person sees one.

The gap can be bridged by imagining a situation that is more severe than what the other person is facing. No matter how optimistic we may be, that optimism has its limits. If we picture ourselves in a situation that pushes us beyond those limits, we will be better able to relate to the situation that pushes the other person beyond his.

EXAMPLE:

Jessica is sitting on the floor of her room, concentrating intensely. The task of tying her shoelaces always gives her difficulty. She has succeeded at it on a handful of occasions, but the two cords that she is holding with her fingers are giving her so much trouble that she finds it hard to remember them now. Finally, she yanks them in frustration and starts crying.

Watching this, her mother starts feeling frustrated herself. She's told Jessica many times that, if she needs help, she just needs to ask. She's a small girl and still has a lot to learn. She can't expect to get it all right at her age. She may as well come to terms with it. Crying about it is definitely not going to help her.

Instead of verbalizing her frustration, the mother makes another attempt at understanding what her daughter is going through. She thinks of the challenges that she is facing in her own life. A recent attempt at ice-skating comes to mind. She had never ice skated in her life, until a group of friends invited her to come with them and try it out, promising loads of fun. She did, not expecting to measure up to them on her first attempt but just looking to spend some fun time together.

The first tumble came as no surprise to her. The ice was much more slippery than she anticipated and the balance more difficult to keep. She also took the next few falls in her stride. As the session went on, however, and her skill didn't noticeably improve, she started to get frustrated. Her friends' words of comfort and encouragement didn't help. She kept looking at their practiced turns and comparing them with her own fledgling efforts. Outwardly she was full of praise for their skill and understanding of her own first tentative steps in this direction. Inwardly, she felt like a failure.

Recalling this experience helps her better understand what her daughter is going through. When one repeatedly fails at a task, words of sympathy and encouragement from people who have succeeded at it can mean very little. Instead of giving her daughter another piece of advice on what she can do in preference to crying, she just hugs her in understanding.

The second skill that we need to cultivate is the examination of personal experience. As was explained earlier in the book, we need to be able to identify the emotional state that we are in, determine how circumstances and our reaction to them have conspired to produce it, and evaluate its desirability. We need to do this so that we can tell how we would like other people to treat us.

What these two skills give us is intimate familiarity with the experiences that we have lived through, and adequate grasp of the experience that another person is currently going through. What we need now is a bridge between the two, a way to bring them together so that we can draw on our past experience when deciding how best to respond to the situation that the other person is presently experiencing. This might seem obvious – we just treat him the way we would like him to treat us. There is a snag, however.

The complication is that different people have different tastes and preferences. If we ignore this difference, we will try to impose our tastes and preferences on other people, with disastrous results[9]. What we need to do in an effort to avoid this is to convert our personal experience into a general form. In other words, we need to look beneath our individual preferences to identify the overarching desires – the desire for freedom of choice, understanding, fair treatment, equality of opportunity, and yes, the desire to have our individual preferences respected.

Applying these skills together enables us to unleash the power of our personal experience to bear on the present situation in such a way that other people benefit from our involvement, even if they were unable or unwilling to tell us exactly how they would like us to treat them, and even if they didn't know themselves. This is the essence of the Golden Rule – *do unto others as you would have them do unto you.*

We apply the skills by relying on empathy to grant us insight into what another person is experiencing, generalizing their experience into overarching desires that we hopefully share, and then drawing on our examined personal experience to decide how we would like them to treat us if the roles were reversed. Then we treat them that way.

---

[9] This is George Bernard Shaw's criticism of the Golden Rule when he says "Do not do unto others as you would expect they should do unto you. Their tastes may not be the same."

EXAMPLE:

The family gathering was in full swing. Henry loved seeing all of the members of the extended family assembled together. It was important to him to spend time with them and catch up with the events in their lives, even his niece and nephew, who he saw were at each other's throats again. Perhaps it was good that they didn't see each other too often. She knew how to push his buttons, and he wasn't always able to keep his reaction under control.

Realizing that other family members were watching them, they moved their argument to one of the unoccupied rooms inside the house. Henry followed them, concerned that the matter may get out of hand, as it had before. His concern was well grounded. No sooner did they think they were out of sight of other people than they let rip. His niece had some choice things to say to his nephew. Henry was astounded at the venom with which she said them and how she took obvious delight in provoking him to the point where he lost control. He tried to lash back at her. Unable to compete verbally, he followed this up with a physical assault.

Henry was taken aback by the turn of events. He didn't expect it to go this far. As much as his niece loved provoking his nephew until he lost his composure, Henry was quite sure that she didn't want to be hit. And as much as his nephew was determined to get back at her in whatever way he could, Henry knew from personal experience that going too far, as appealing as it may have been in the heat of the argument, would be regretted later. He jumped in the tussle and pulled them apart, doing his best to act in their mutual best interest.

Reading this, we might get the impression that following the Golden Rule requires us to invest a great deal of time and effort before we can decide how to act in any given situation. This will be the case if we are utterly unfamiliar with the process. Like with any skill, however, the more we practice it, the more proficient we become at applying it. Empathy, in particular, can be developed to such an extent that using it becomes an automatic aspect of interacting with other people.

Trial and Error

Guidelines for appreciating the possibilities in a given situation only go so far. They are all ultimately curtailed by the availability of personal experience. If we have never freely satisfied the needs of another person, we might not anticipate that doing so would give us the experience of abundance. If we have never hurt others in an outburst of anger, we might not realize that preventing another person from doing so against his will would be appreciated later, when he has had time to calm down and take stock of the situation.

When presented with a new situation that is quite unlike any we have ever been in, the best course of action might be to take the plunge and see how it pans out. Doing so can help broaden our horizons. It will certainly give us new experience to evaluate. This can serve as a basis for choosing how to act when subsequent similar situations present themselves.

EXAMPLE:

It is evening. Charles is about to take a shower. He's got his things ready – a towel to dry himself with and the clothes that he is going to put on afterwards. The soap and shampoo are resting at their customary places. He steps inside the shower and closes the door. Then the power goes out.

Standing in the dark, he can feel his frustration mounting. He can get back out and stumble across the room to grab hold of some candles or a lantern. Then he can wait for the lights to come back on so that he can enjoy the shower, or have a bath by candlelight instead. However, having gone to all the trouble of getting ready and stopping just short of turning the water on, he decides that he may as well go through with what he has started. He proceeds to have a shower in the dark.

After a short while, his eyes adjust to make use of what little moonlight is streaming in through the window. He is familiar enough with his surroundings to locate the soap and shampoo without much trouble. He soon discovers that darkness doesn't present him with much of an obstacle. In fact, it adds an important dimension to the overall experience, one whose absence he has never noticed before.

With his eyes deprived of sensation and his ears dulled by the monotonous sound of falling water, he finds his sense of touch respond with heightened awareness. His whole body tingles from the gentle massaging of the water cascading over it. Starved of its usual sensory input, his mind looks for something else to occupy itself with. Combined with the relaxed state of his body, it becomes unusually receptive to flashes of insight.

Not having showered in the dark before, Charles could only anticipate what it might be like by taking away the convenience of eyesight from his usual shower experience. He could not foresee the benefits of sensory deprivation. Having experienced it once, his attitude towards it changes and he decides to make showering in the dark a part of his daily routine.

EXAMPLE:

Sandra recently moved into a new house. It was a modest-sized place. The building rubble that covered the back yard was removed shortly before she moved in, exposing raw earth beneath it. She wondered what to do with it. She wasn't one for gardening, but she also didn't want to leave the yard like that, waiting to be taken over by weeds.

One day, while shopping, she came across packets of seeds for various vegetables that could be grown on small plots and even in pots. They intrigued her. She had never grown vegetables before – she assumed it involved a lot of backbreaking labor – but the prospect of trying her hand at it played on her mind. Acting on impulse, she bought the few seed packets that could be planted this time of year and took them home.

With no background in farming and not a great deal of free time to play around with, she roughly delineated a few vegetable patches – careful to leave sufficient walking space between them – threw the seeds over them and covered them with a thin layer of well matured organic compost that she had also bought.

Over the next few days, she left the garden alone, except for making sure that it was adequately watered. The seeds that she had planted grew in a haphazard pattern, accompanied by several species of weeds. She didn't have much time for weeding, so she only cut back or pulled out the biggest ones. Much to her surprise, the vegetables didn't seem to mind the presence of weeds too much. Thanks to the moist fertile soil, they grew and prospered.

Sandra soon found herself attracted to the garden. Unexpectedly to her, some of the vegetables produced beautiful flowers. She ran her fingers across the fruit that they turned into. She particularly liked the feel of the inside of the broad bean casing. It was velvety and exquisite to touch. Picking her first vegetables to prepare a meal was a delightful experience, one that completely transformed the way she looked at gardening.

Because she didn't depend on the vegetable garden to supply her with food, there was no stress associated with tending it. She could put in as much effort as she wanted to, and use whatever food it was able to produce. She could also get creative and plant the seeds in whatever pattern she desired, without having to take heed of the best farming practices.

As seasons went on, she started spending more time in the garden. She found herself drawn to it. There was a living quality to it that was markedly absent from the rest of her property. She could almost feel the triumph of seedlings as they broke through the ground cover to have their first taste of sunlight. She shared in the joy of cabbage leaves as they soaked up the moisture from a light summer rain. Having an intimate connection with nature added a dimension to her existence that she never knew was missing from her life.

Projection

The section Empathy has briefly touched on a constraint that we face when trying to choose the most beneficial course of action in a given situation. That constraint is our own mental or emotional state. Put simply, our moods color our interpretation of events, and, in so doing, influence our experience.

If we approach a situation with a negative mindset, we might altogether fail to appreciate the possibilities inherent in it. The decisions that would ordinarily unleash the most desirable consequences won't even occur to us, or will appear so obviously undesirable that we won't seriously entertain the notion of making them.

EXAMPLE:

Even though John could see the difficulty of the woman's circumstances, the thought of parting with some of his hard-earned money stopped him in his tracks. His job entailed a lot of hard work that wasn't paid well. There were bills he had to pay and the family's needs he had to attend to. Giving away small change to a beggar woman wouldn't make much of a difference, but how many more times will he be expected to do that? He broke off the eye contact with the woman and faced forward, sitting uncomfortably in his car and waiting for the traffic light to change. It felt like an eternity, though it was only seconds before he was able to drive off.

His inaction amounted to the statement that he had so little that he couldn't afford to share any of it. Again it didn't matter how rich or poor he was relative to the people that he knew and associated with. He experienced poverty by the simple act of holding on to his possessions when he could see that their sharing was desperately needed.

Even if we succeed at recognizing the possibilities in a situation and choosing a course of action that purportedly yields the most desirable experience, we may fail to have this experience if we hold on to thoughts that diminish it.

EXAMPLE:

Seeing the difficulty of the woman's circumstances, John reached for the money that was in his car to give some of it to her. As he was doing that, a thought popped into his mind: this was a lot of money to part with. He couldn't afford to give it away. There were bills that had to be paid and his own needs that needed looking after. The misgivings continued playing on his mind even as he was giving the money away.

Even though he acted generously, he had an experience of scarcity due to holding on to the thought that he couldn't really afford to do so.

For the guidelines described in this chapter to be of benefit to us, we have to ensure that we are able to take advantage of the most beneficial courses of action that they offer. This requires our outlook to be sufficiently open to recognize the potential for these choices in the present circumstances, and sufficiently positive that we don't feel a sense of loss once we make them.

Summary: Questions to Ask Myself

Pertaining to circumstantial potential:
Can I grasp the possibilities inherent in the present circumstances?
Can I identify more desirable circumstances that the present situation can lead to?

Can I relate to other people and what they are going through?

How do I cultivate a positive mindset?

Experimenting with Beliefs

"Habits of thought persist through the centuries; and while a healthy brain may reject the doctrine it no longer believes, it will continue to feel the same sentiments formerly associated with that doctrine."
Charlotte Perkins Gilman

I have delayed the discussion of beliefs until this point because they are considerably more difficult to get to grips with than words, actions, or goals. Even thoughts and feelings present fewer obstacles. In fact, beliefs are so different that it is not clear that we can even get to grips with them at all, at least not to anywhere near the same extent.

The section <u>Overcoming False Internalized Beliefs</u> described how to overcome the limitations of presently held beliefs. The process consists of acting on impulse and paying attention to the resulting experience. This enables us to dislodge beliefs that contradict that experience. Such beliefs serve to our detriment. The ability to break free of their restrictions is invaluable.

However, this is a far cry from choosing to adopt beliefs that we find desirable, as we can do with goals and actions.

There are additional factors that have to be considered for this to be a possibility. This chapter delves into the unique nature of beliefs to discover how they work and how they can be put to work for us in a deliberate manner.

The Nature of Beliefs

Beliefs comprise the framework within which we live our lives. This framework tells us what our environment consists of and how it functions, who we are and how we fit inside it, what it all means, what its purpose is, what is possible and not possible, and literally every other aspect of our existence.

For beliefs to be able to play such a commanding role, they have to meet some hefty requirements. Firstly, as the term suggests, they have to be believable. Because we have criteria for what makes them believable to us, we cannot disregard those criteria when adopting new beliefs. This would amount to pretending that we believe something that we distinctly know we don't. Such an attempt would produce views that we don't find believable, and are therefore unable to incorporate into our worldview, regardless of how much we may like them and want to make use of them.

Secondly, to be effective, the framework of beliefs must be internally consistent. Whenever one belief is changed, there is a risk of unsettling the rest, so that the structure as a whole becomes in danger of collapsing. While there are ways to soften the requirement for coherency – rationalization can be surprisingly effective at allowing two contradictory beliefs to coexist within the same worldview – they have their limitations. These limitations are exacerbated whenever contradictions are brought out into the open, as deliberate living strives to do.

Acquisition of Beliefs

Acquisition of beliefs begins in early childhood and continues for the remainder of our lives. It is partly rooted in experience and partly derived from various authority figures – peers, parents, teachers, celebrities, priests, scientists, philosophers – who feature prominently in our lives and whose work exerts a definitive influence on the way we perceive the world and ourselves.

Much of this process, especially during childhood and adolescence, proceeds unconsciously. We learn by observation – we come to see the world the way we perceive others to see it, and relate to it the way they do. By the time we are mature enough to carve our own path through life, we have already constructed an elaborate belief framework from borrowed material. This framework guides our decisions even as we are busy deciding how to alter it.

The beliefs that comprise this framework have different degrees of visibility. Some of them are quite explicit and readily subjected to validation. Beliefs that promptly follow from observations made by the physical senses are a good example. Being burned by a hot stove gives us a good reason to keep away from all kinds of hot objects without having to repeat the experience with each one in turn. If we hold a contrary belief, dispensing with it is a simple matter of acquainting ourselves with the relevant hot object through touch.

Some beliefs lurk beneath the surface and only betray their presence by the influence that they have on other beliefs. If we believe that everyone should earn their keep, this is not likely to manifest directly, but only through the beliefs that it gives rise to – that working adults must plan for their retirement, that beggars should not be given charity, etc. This makes them more difficult to inspect. We can still do so by acting on impulse and examining the resulting experience, as described in the earlier chapter.

Some beliefs are buried so deeply within our worldview, with so many layers of beliefs placed on top of them that it is very difficult for us to realize that they even exist, let alone assess their soundness. Like axioms that form the foundation of scientific practice, their validity is self-evident to us. So self-evident, in fact, that they often manage to pass unnoticed. For example, the belief that many objects that can be found in our surroundings – such as rocks and metals – are inanimate is so obvious that it doesn't even occur to us to question it. It is only when we are exposed to people who hold fundamentally different views, typically those from other cultures, that we even become aware of them.

There is another important difference between these hidden beliefs and the highly visible ones, such as those that caution us about the danger of coming into contact with hot objects. The beliefs that rest at the foundation of our worldview are remarkably difficult to verify. Different people can have radically different basic ideas about how the world works without their behavior betraying the fact that their model of reality is utterly mistaken.

Acting on impulse will not help us here. Whatever experience this generates will typically be incorporated into the current worldview with only minor adjustments having to be made. The base of that worldview will not be brought into question.

EXAMPLE:

As a mining engineer with a hefty amount of experience, Robert took great pride in his work. He was well acquainted with the progress that human society has made as a result of technological advancement, and mining has been an essential ingredient of that. From the dawn of civilization, the ability to extract valuable resources from beneath the Earth's surface has enabled the production of increasingly more sophisticated metals, and lately plastics and many other kinds of materials as well. These accomplishments were fitting to a species that has come to dominate all other life forms on Earth and shape its environment to its advantage.

Much to his consternation, Robert has recently become aware of another side to this story of progress. The devastation brought to ecosystems as a result of it has reached such levels that many people, even experts in the field, are questioning human ability to rise to the challenge while continuing with the same damaging practices. Some are also pondering the wisdom of doing so regardless of its viability, bringing into question the very idea that humans are superior and in charge of nature, and are entitled to do with it as they please.

The latter group Robert had no patience with. Of course humans were entitled to use the Earth's resources as they saw fit. They have earned that right by winning the evolutionary struggle to arrive at the top of the food chain. The former group had a point, though. It worried him that humanity has been careless in its domination of nature, and that it had to wait for its technology to develop further. Only then will it be able to safely put its well-earned mastery of nature to good use.

Purposefully altering these embedded beliefs is a formidable challenge. Our experience attests to their validity. The wisdom of our culture holds them to be true. The structure of our worldview rests on their presence. Barring a new and profound contrary experience, it doesn't appear that we can have any say in whether to adopt them or not, regardless of their usefulness.

Making Peace with Contradictions

A way to overcome these difficulties is to notice that we have the capacity to accommodate more than one worldview at the same time. Beliefs that we have acquired through intellectual pursuits might be quite different from those that actually inform our behavior. It could be argued that the beliefs that govern our behavior are the ones that we actually hold and that the others are just something that we wish we had. While this may be true in some cases, I don't think that it is true in general.

One example to this effect has to do with the question of "Free Will". It is common within the scientific establishment to embrace a deterministic view of the world, one that leaves no room for free will. Free will comes to be regarded as merely an illusion. It effectively fools us into thinking that we are at the helm of our lives, when in reality they are entirely a product of external factors.

There is nothing comforting about this view. People who hold it typically don't do so because of its emotional appeal, but because this is where their intellectual examination of the subject has taken them. It is not an ad hoc belief, but one that integrates seamlessly into their worldview. As such, it has to fulfill the requirements for believability and consistency in order to be adopted.

Of the people who hold this belief, I'm not aware of any who actually conduct themselves as if they had no free will. It is easy to see why. Doing away with free will renders many of the concepts that form the fabric of our lives meaningless. It renders the subject of this book meaningless. Living this way would be so self-defeating that it is not even attempted.

As a result, different worldviews are adopted for different purposes – one based on determinism to help them make sense of the world and one endorsing free will to guide their interaction with it. Which belief is professed as valid depends on where we look for the answer.

This is not a temporary inconsistency that the people try to explain away or eliminate as soon as it is brought to their attention. They are generally aware of such contradictions between worldviews and don't perceive them as a problem. They have learned to live with the contradiction.

Purposefully Adopting Beliefs

Having the capacity to accommodate more than one worldview at a time supplies us with the means of overcoming the unique challenges that beliefs present us with. Because the context of the challenge is the adoption of beliefs that will have a positive effect on our behavior, and so in turn enhance our experience, they don't have to meet the same stringent requirements for believability and coherency of the beliefs that we rely on to make sense of the world we live in. This makes it possible to adopt beliefs strictly for the purpose of evaluation[10].

It might not be obvious why we need to adopt beliefs in order to evaluate their desirability. After all, the perceived advantages of the belief are the very reason that we are even considering its adoption. Why won't a purely intellectual examination of its benefits and drawbacks suffice?

It might suffice if it can be done in isolation, if the prospective new belief can be adopted without impacting the beliefs that we already hold. However, this is not usually the case. Such an action displaces the contradictory belief that we already hold and perturbs some others. This turns it into a contest between the new belief and the presently held beliefs that contradict it, to see which is better.

Presently held beliefs have a sizeable advantage in this comparison. Because they govern our thoughts, words and actions, and these in turn produce experience, we have a visceral sense of the effect that these beliefs have on our lives. Intellectual evaluation of competing beliefs pales in comparison. It only has a chance if the emotions that our current beliefs generate are negative, and replacing them with any beneficial beliefs constitutes an improvement.

By adopting a prospective new belief, we give it an opportunity to affect our lives in a manner similar to our current beliefs. As it generates experience, we compare it with the experiences that our prior beliefs have produced to see which is the more desirable. The process comes to completion once we have experienced the consequences of the new belief suf-

---

[10] This essentially faith-based approach stands in stark contrast with William Kingdon Clifford's view that "...it is wrong always, everywhere, and for anyone, to believe anything upon insufficient evidence."

ficiently to get a measure of it that sets it apart from the beliefs that were previously held.

EXAMPLE:

Watching an assault on another man's integrity was a life-changing event for Nancy. She was attending a company-sponsored workshop with a handful of work colleagues. They were sitting in a commons area enjoying coffee and biscuits during the mid-morning break when she noticed an irate woman venting her anger at one of the trainers from the adjacent workshop venue. Even from a distance, she could hear what the woman was saying. It wasn't pleasant or even respectful. She was having a full go at the trainer and everything that he stood for.

To Nancy's surprise, he made no attempt to defend himself. He only stood there, waiting patiently for his attacker to finish. Then he smiled – a warm, compassionate smile – before proceeding to respond. His tone was much too quiet for her to hear what he was saying. She just saw that his words and his demeanor effectively disarmed his assailant. They exchanged a few more words, and then the woman extended a gesture of reconciliation and promptly left.

Nancy had no knowledge of the background to the incident, but what she saw impressed her to such an extent that she knew she wanted what that man had. She appreciated his ability to diffuse an explosive situation and wished it for herself.

She mulled the incident over in her mind for the remainder of the day. Once the workshops were finished, she went across to the other trainer's room. She expressed her admiration for his earlier conduct and wanted to know how he was able to handle the situation so calmly and constructively. He proceeded to explain that he subscribed to a belief system that saw no division between different objects that comprised their environment. There was unity to existence that manifested itself in different forms. When the woman approached him, he saw her as an aspect of himself that was in distress and he did what he could to comfort her and alleviate her anguish, because he understood that, in so doing, he was merely comforting himself.

Nancy could understand how his belief could sponsor such behavior, even though the belief itself made no sense to her. It was clearly false. We were all distinct biological organisms. This was patently obvious. Still, the demonstration that she had seen had a profound effect. She wasn't prepared to forgo its benefits, even if the belief that gave rise to it was nonsensical. She decided that she was going to try it out in the hope that it would hold some benefit for her too.

When she got home, she found that her husband was upset with her for being late. Rather than defend her delay or rebuke him for his impatience, she tried to look at him as an aspect of herself that has just experienced a different set of circumstances. To be able to do that, she had to know what those circumstances were. She realized that the supper was late and noticed that the kids were out of hand. Judging by the papers that were spread out over the desk, her husband still had some unfinished work to attend to. No wonder he was short-tempered. Her response rooted in the newly found understanding, she proceeded to reassure him, quickly put some snacks together and take care of the kids.

With time, she found that this outlook on life worked in a wide variety of situations. Self-identifying with another person or object brought out the best in her. She treated them with all the care and understanding that she quite naturally extended to herself. It didn't matter that she didn't hold this belief intellectually; her behavior became intentionally conditioned by it to such an extent that it unfolded spontaneously.

EXAMPLE:

Kyle has spent much of his early adulthood working out the details of the religion that he wholeheartedly believed in. Its message was critically important, so he did his best to make other people aware of it, and whatever he could to help them embrace it and live according to its principles. Many people disagreed with his beliefs and his eagerness to share them, even going so far as to describe him as dogmatic and label him a fundamentalist, but he persevered against the obstacles that they placed in his way.

That is, until he started having doubts about his own belief system. Taking up their challenge, he thoroughly explored the foundation on which his worldview rested – and found it wanting. A strongly rational person, he was horrified to discover that a lot of the beliefs that he had taken for granted were nothing more than articles of faith. Profoundly unsettled by what he had uncovered, he underwent a fundamental revision of his belief system to purge it of everything that he couldn't verify to his satisfaction. He became an atheist.

Stepping out of the religion that he had grown up with enabled him to look at it in an entirely different light. His new mission became to help the people who shared in his former work see their beliefs the way he saw them now, and embrace his new worldview in their place. Many of the people who opposed him in the past now supported him on his new quest, while his former allies criticized him for a closed-minded rejection of the self-evident truths that still formed the foundation of their lives. He didn't let their resistance discourage him, though. The work of helping them shed their erroneous beliefs and see the world the way he did was much too important to be abandoned so easily.

Some years later, he found himself resting in a hospital bed while recovering from a minor surgery. The patient lying in the bed next to him was in a much more serious condition. It wasn't clear whether he would survive. He was an atheist, like Kyle, only a lifelong one. The likelihood of his death brought a whole host of existential questions out to the surface, many of which he hadn't seriously engaged until now. It was a disquieting prospect. Kyle wanted to help him with his dilemma, but found himself uncharacteristically at a loss for words.

He was almost relieved to see the man's wife walk in. It was visiting hours at the hospital and she checked in every day to see how her husband was doing and to offer him whatever support and encouragement she could. Last night had been particularly trying. The pain was difficult to bear. Coupled with the grim prognosis, it just seemed utterly pointless. Overcome with despair, he broke down in her arms and started crying.

It was unsettling for Kyle to see the man in this state, especially because he couldn't help him. He knew that the man's wife was religious. This was the perfect opportunity for her to impress her beliefs on her husband, taking advantage of his moment of weakness.

To Kyle's astonishment, she did none of that. She knew him so well, and loved him so much, that she gave him all the support that she could from within the boundaries of his own belief system. It was her respect for her husband that drove her to treat the beliefs that he had embraced with all the courtesy that she could muster, as much as she may have disagreed with them.

Her example shook Kyle to the core. All the arguments about beliefs that he had engaged in over the years suddenly seemed so trivial. He perceived with unmistakable clarity that what mattered at the end of the day was not how accurate his model of the world was, but how he treated those around him. And he was distraught to admit that he had frequently allowed his quest for truth to get in the way of his humanity.

Even though his ailment was minor, he left the hospital a different person. His worldview hadn't changed; he still believed that its basic assumptions were correct, even if the details needed some work. However, proclaiming its truth no longer occupied the center stage in his life. He shared it when he thought it was appropriate, always mindful of how much his audience wanted to hear it, and careful to soften the impact according to what he thought they could deal with. While his model of reality remained unchanged, the extent to which it influenced his behavior was radically altered.

Summary: Questions to Ask Myself

What discrepancies exist between beliefs that I use to make sense of the world and beliefs that guide my interaction with it?

What beliefs form the base of each worldview that I hold?

Regarding foundational beliefs:
Which ones would I rather hold?
How do I adopt them?

Living Deliberately

Putting It All Together

"Well-makers lead the water; archers bend the bow; carpenters hew a log of wood; wise people fashion themselves."

Hazrat Inayat Khan

Thus far, part two of the book has explored our conduct in the form of words and actions, the thoughts that sponsor it, the feelings that it produces, the circumstances in which it is expressed and the beliefs that constrain it. We have looked at how to identify the consequences of our actions as well as how to evaluate them. Lastly, we have sought to extend our knowledge beyond the realm of our own experience so as to fast track our growth. What remains to be seen is how all of these concepts come together to shape our daily lives.

One way to do this is to picture a traditional time line – with distinct segments for the past, the present, and the future – and place the various concepts and activities in their appropriate time slot. After this is done, all that remains is to see how they interact to make this approach to living come alive.

The Role of the Past

The past acts as a repository of information regarding our conduct. It is by looking into our past that we discover how we have conducted ourselves on previous occasions and how successful this conduct has been. The evaluation of this information is critical if we are to make reasonable decisions on which aspects of our behavior need to change and in what way.

There is a trivial yet vitally important observation that can be made. Everything that has ever happened resides in the past – all the circumstances and all the people's actions, including our own. Even acts that have been committed only moments ago belong there. This makes it impossible to determine what a person is like by examining her actions. We can only conclude what she *was* like.

This has tremendous implications on the way we live our lives. To get a sense of them, it helps to notice that our past conduct invariably contains errors in judgment, and that these errors tend to impose a burden of guilt. Indeed, it is a common practice in our society to emphasize this burden in an effort to make the magnitude of the mistake abundantly clear to the person who has committed it.

As effective as guilt can be in highlighting our errors, it has an unfortunate side-effect – it keeps us trapped in those errors. This is done by bringing the past judgments into the present. Instead of relying on the past to guide our future conduct, we allow it to completely define that conduct, and with it us as well. This makes it tremendously difficult to correct the mistakes that have brought on the guilt in the first place.

Even if we do correct the mistakes and act desirably on subsequent occasions, the guilt often persists. Even atoning for what we have done might not be enough. Once embraced, guilt is not easily let go. This is why the most effective way to deal with it is not to embrace it in the first place.

If our conduct does not automatically define who we are, but only who we were at the time when we engaged in it, then the weight of its implications cannot be automatically applied to us in the present tense either. We can still choose to accept the implications, including guilt, if we find value in them. However, this is our decision to make. It cannot be imposed from the outside without our consent.

The Role of the Future

Since the past does not define who we are, we need to look for our identity elsewhere. The future is a more suitable source. In this context, the future can be thought of as unrealized potential. It is not about trying to anticipate the future – ascertaining what will or might happen at some future date and time – but about seeing what has the potential to happen. It is about exploring possibilities so that we can decide which ones to manifest.

The future complements the past in helping us chart the course forward. The past guides the future – our past failures tell us where we need to seek a grander vision, while our past successes indicate where we are on course and shouldn't expect to find more than minor improvements. Because the future amounts to unrealized potential, it gives us a free license to conceive anything that we wish to conceive. It may be guided by our past, but it is only constrained by our imaginations.

EXAMPLE:

After months of being single, Rachel has met someone fascinating at a mutual friend's party. She finds him attractive in more ways than one. What particularly interests her about him is that he treats other people with a great deal of respect. After her previous failed relationship, this was of utmost importance to her.

The previous relationship was a stormy affair. Living through it felt like a rollercoaster ride – a series of alternating emotional highs and lows. She loved the good times, but dreaded the mutual problems that she and her partner experienced and the hurt that they inflicted on each other as a result.

As she thought of the potential new relationship, Rachel was still weary of being hurt. The past wounds had not yet healed. She didn't want to reopen them. Fortunately, all it took was a reminder of her parents' happy union to erase the fears and give her the courage and the strength to plunge ahead in the hope that her love and trust will bear more bountiful fruit than the previous time. She knew deep down that she was not so easy to hurt, and that she had enough love, patience, and forgiveness in her to heal most heartaches.

The Role of the Present

This is where the action takes place. All of the elements that we have explored thus far come together here. We encounter a particular situation and need to decide how to respond to it. Alternatively, we may start with a particular goal that we wish to achieve and seek out appropriate circumstances in an effort to do so.

The purpose of framing our response is to realize – and thereby experience – our idealistic self-perception in the present circumstances. To do so, we draw on our knowledge of desirable goals and the means of attaining them. Then we act out the choices that we have made and experience their consequences.

We can heighten the resulting experience by contrasting it with the memory of past ones. Our memory of the past enables us to place our experience of the present in a larger context. It is through this mechanism that we can get a visceral sense of our evolving natures.

Subsequent analysis of the resulting experience can be used to extend our knowledge base of worthwhile goals, which in turn enhances our idealistic self-perception. Analysis can also extend our knowledge of actions and their consequences, which gives us practical tools with which to manifest the grander self-perception next time a similar situation presents itself.

EXAMPLE:

Tanya looked at her son's self-satisfied grin. He was genuinely pleased with himself. She was tempted to be pleased with him too, though past experience warned her that his source of satisfaction may not meet with her approval. Sure enough, he proceeded to show her the drawing that he had just finished. The work of art measured almost a meter across the passage wall, and was done with a permanent marker. He looked at her, expecting her to admire his considerable creativity.

It took her a moment to come to terms with what she was seeing. She almost went through the roof! She wanted to scream and wallop him across the face, but somehow managed to hold her actions in check. She wasn't able to do so the previous time she was faced with vandalism of her property. The violent reaction did no good, so she was determined to avoid repeating it. She breathed deeply and waited until she was sufficiently calm to address her son in a controlled voice. He knew that mommy wasn't happy and drew very quiet and still, but at least the screaming and crying scene was avoided.

EXAMPLE:

Encouraged by her past success, Tanya resolved to handle the wall painting even more constructively next time around. She knew from her friends' experience that she had likely not seen the last of it. Their warning proved to be accurate. Merely a week later, she spotted a brand new wall painting in her son's room. He was careful not to attract attention to his new work of art this time around, but couldn't quite resist drawing it either.

Unlike the previous times, she was well prepared for it. Instead of venting her fury or tormenting him with strained silence, she sat him down and talked to him about drawing on the walls and why it was wrong. She impressed herself with the amount of restraint that she was able to display.

What she didn't expect was for her son to defend his conduct. He obviously liked what he drew, as inappropriate as it was. Why was it inappropriate, she suddenly wondered? She knew that none of the adults approved of it, but there must have been more to it than mere personal preference. Yet the more she thought about it, the more she realized that there was nothing else. Children liked it; parents were horrified by it. Because parents decided on the rules, drawing on the walls was out of the question.

Stunned by the insight, she grasped that the exemplary behavior that she had just displayed could be improved even further. More than just a mother who patiently kept her children in line, she could allow them to unleash their creative potential when she had no reason to curtail it that extended beyond personal preference. She became aware of a whole new world of possibilities.

EXAMPLE:

Mark is driving along a busy highway on his way home from work. It's been a hectic day. He is looking forward to a warm supper and some quiet time with his family. As he is driving, he notices a car stationed next to the highway. It appears to have broken down. The hood is up, with a man tinkering underneath it. Another is standing next to him and signaling to the ongoing traffic that they are in need of a ride.

Mark could understand their predicament. If their day has been anything like his, they would greatly prefer resting at home to being stranded by the highway. To make matters worse, it was going to be dark soon. He had a natural tendency to go out of his way to help people when he could see that help was needed. He was proud of this trait of his and derived tremendous satisfaction from it.

As he was about to turn off the highway, he remembered the stories that he had heard about people who had stopped to offer hitchhikers a ride, only to be assaulted by them. Some of these were deliberate traps set up to lure unsuspecting passer-byes. The two people that he saw standing by the road seemed genuine enough, but how could he tell? There were two of them whereas he was alone. If they attacked him, would he be able to resist?

The concerns about security prevailed. He continued the slow drive along the congested highway. He still knew that he was a helpful person. Unfortunately, he failed to experience what he knew to be true about himself, and so did the two people who were left stranded by the road.

To be clear, the above process doesn't proceed in smooth, calculated fashion where we perform a lengthy analysis and look at a situation from every angle before making a decision. We generally don't have the luxury of doing so. Many situations that we encounter require us to respond promptly. Be it confronting someone's upsetting behavior, consoling a person in distress, acting courteously in traffic, providing a suitable example for youngsters, or a myriad other situations, the opportunity for action only presents itself for a few moments. If we miss it, our indecision will itself amount to a reaction — that we condone someone's behavior, do not wish to comfort them, and so on.

For this reason, in many situations, we cannot rely on analysis of the present circumstances to tell us how to behave. That decision follows from past analyses of situations that bore sufficient similarity to the present to serve as a suitable guide. In addition to the challenge of performing accurate analysis, we have the challenge of identifying an appropriate analysis to rely on, and even remembering to use it to override our established pattern of behavior when prior analysis shows it to be faulty.

These challenges are formidable. It takes time to get to grips with changes of this nature, even when they are obviously desirable. Our present behavior is likely a product of a great deal of repetition, conscious or not. We cannot reasonably expect to overhaul it in a single attempt. This is why it helps to make peace with the fact that we will continue to stumble on our way, reassured by the knowledge that our stumbling is moving us closer to our goal, and that every step that we take, however flawed, brings its own reward.

Summary: Questions to Ask Myself

What is my idealistic self-perception?

When Things Fall Apart

"A good education is not so much one which prepares a man to succeed in the world, as one which enables him to sustain a failure."
Bernard Iddings Bell

Thus far, we have examined individual elements of the process of deliberate living and we have seen how they come together to make it possible. Hopefully this has given us a good idea of the effects that this approach to living is able to produce and some sense of their desirability. What remains to be seen is what to do when it doesn't work out as we'd hoped.

Deliberate living is no safeguard against failure. It helps us in some ways – by encouraging us to take heed of the consequences of our actions, learn from the behavior of others, and so on – but it works against us as well – by taking us into unexplored territory in order to learn and grow. Making mistakes somewhere along the line is unavoidable. It is best to come to terms with this fact and learn how to live with them.

Before we begin, we need to be clear that failure as defined here is not the same as the common usage of the term – failing exams, getting fired, divorce, etc. These failures are the result of not meeting social norms. Deliberate living is not constrained by social norms, so failure in this context is correspondingly different. Broadly, there are two ways in which we can fail — by choosing wrong goals, and by failing to achieve the goals that we have set for ourselves.

The Importance of Intention

The way we live our lives tends to be goal-oriented. When we engage in action, it is typically with the goal of accomplishing something. We sow seeds in a garden to help it grow in a particular way; we study a particular field of endeavor to prepare us for future participation in that field; we put in the time and the effort to listen to our friends' difficulties to console them, encourage them, and help them overcome those obstacles.

On the other hand, many of the teachings that deal with spiritual pursuits tend to highlight the drawbacks of attachment to results. They correctly point out that we cannot control the circumstances to the extent that is needed to ensure that our goals are reached. If the sole purpose of our engaging in an activity is to achieve a particular end result, we are likely to make a substantial emotional investment in achieving that result. If we fail, even if the circumstances were beyond our control, we are nevertheless bound to feel disappointed. If the seeds do not grow due to lack of rain, the studies do not give us the grounding that we need, or our friends decline to heed our advice, we will fail to reach our goals. If reaching these goals was the sole motivation for our actions, it would be all too easy to feel that we have wasted our time and that our efforts have been futile.

The approach that is presented in this book offers a different underlying motive. Instead of engaging in activities in order to achieve particular goals, our conduct can simply be an expression of who we are. If we value abundant plant growth and have a preference for certain types of plants, sowing seeds in a garden is a way of expressing this value and these preferences. If we have an interest in a particular field of endeavor, we can express this interest by learning about that field. If we genuinely care for our friends, we will demonstrate this caring by helping, consoling, and encouraging them.

There is no real difference between the two approaches with respect to their external manifestation. The seeds will grow just the same, our studies will progress the same way and our conduct towards our friends will be the same. What is different is the effect that this behavior can have on us. By basing our motivation on our self-perception, we free ourselves from dependency on circumstances that lie beyond our control. Our sense of accomplishment is instead derived solely from our intention and whether it was worthwhile.

EXAMPLE:

Gary was sitting next to his friend, his hand on the man's shoulder in a gesture of silent reassurance. This followed another fall out with his girlfriend, who was emotionally abusing him. Gary and his friend had been in this situation several times before. He knew that things weren't likely to change this time around either, and that his friend was probably going to resume the relationship without addressing the underlying issues. Whatever advice he had to offer him was likely to go unheeded.

Nevertheless, Gary did his best to offer words of advice, encouragement, and support. He was surprised to discover that the very act of doing so was immensely rewarding. He knew that he did the best he could to help his friend deal with the problem. He would love to see him follow the advice, but this was not what made it worthwhile. The very act of giving what he could to a friend in need was its own reward.

It may be tempting to conclude that, as long as our actions are motivated by the right intentions, we shouldn't be perturbed by unintended results that they produce. This is true with respect to the common usage of the word *result* – succeeding or failing at growing plants, qualifying for a job or consoling a friend. We gain nothing from being unsettled by factors outside of our control.

However, this is not the only kind of result that actions produce. As long as we are aware of the consequences of our actions, those actions will generate experience that we will not be able to escape. This is most clearly illustrated with the last of the three examples. While we may not derive our sense of worth from whether we have succeeded at consoling a friend but only from the well intentioned attempts at doing so, if our friend remains disheartened, we will share in his distress by virtue of paying attention to his emotional state. We will not necessarily go through what he is going through, but his anguish will not leave us unaffected.

Not Accomplishing Tasks

Of the failures that we have to contend with, this one occurs at the earliest stage of the process. We set our heart and mind to accomplishing a certain task and then find that we are unable to do so. This could be because we lack the talent to master it, the determination to see it through, or a whole host of other reasons.

Of the types of failure that we can encounter, this one is perhaps the most damaging to one's self-esteem. It is the most likely to lead to the simple and devastating conclusion that one *is* a failure, rather than that one has misunderstood, miscalculated, or committed some other such oversight.

When confronting it, it is important to distinguish between two different kinds of tasks that we might find ourselves failing at. The first kind could be described as genuine failure. For example, if our crops don't grow and we need them to feed us, we have a serious problem on our hands. No amount of positive thinking is going to make it disappear. Even in this instance, however, it is helpful to focus on the task at hand and pour all our energy into finding an alternative solution instead of being distracted by negative emotions that are typically associated with failure. This will be explored in the section <u>Mastering Failure</u>.

The second kind of failure arises from our interpretation of what we perceive to be unfavorable developments. This type of failure occurs with much greater frequency than the first. Fortunately, it can be made to disappear with a change in perception.

Having breezed through high school – getting good grades with minimal effort – I enrolled for the study of electrical engineering at the local university. After a good start, I found myself unexpectedly struggling with many of the subjects, eventually failing for two consecutive years (I failed much worse the second time around, despite having fewer subjects). It took me a long time to come to terms with these events.

Once I did, I was able to learn a great deal about myself from this important experience. Looking back, it was the most valuable lesson of my whole education.

The first step in changing the perception is to decrease the importance that we currently attach to the task that we have failed at.[11] When I deregistered from the Faculty of Engineering and was looking to enroll for the study of computer science, I was desperate to make the transfer in a way that minimized the duration of the course, so that I could get my degree as soon as possible. The professor whom I spoke to couldn't quite suppress his amusement. He had seen many other students in my position, no doubt. It was only when my attitude changed from completing the studies as quickly as possible to enjoying them and doing the best I could that my academic success returned.

Removing the attainment of results from their pedestal paves the way for a shift in approach, one that turns the focus away from end results and towards the intention with which they are pursued, as described in the previous section.

With end results no longer looming so large in our sights, we have an easier time transferring our attention to a different set of results, a different task that we wish to master, or some other activity that we find more enjoyable. It took me four years to realize that electrical engineering was not for me and that what I really wanted to do was computer science. Once I came to terms with this fact, I could understand and let go of my prior failure.

---

[11] This sentiment is eloquently captured by Ethel Barrymore's words "You grow up the day you have your first real laugh at yourself."

Misunderstanding Cause and Effect

The next kind of failure that we can encounter takes place once we accomplish the task that we have set out to do, only to discover that it does not produce the outcome that we have hoped to achieve. This occurs due to lack of understanding of cause and effect. Learning about it often proceeds by trial and error. Because the principles are tricky to apply and work within the vast domain of personal experience, we can expect this kind of failure to be a frequent companion.

EXAMPLE:

As a devoted mother of two small boys, Sarah was determined to bring them up to be respectful, well-behaved adults. To this end, she was careful not to tolerate ill-disciplined behavior that they occasionally engaged in, scolding them for it, and resorting to spanking when this didn't work. She saw them misbehave less and less and was happy with the results of her efforts in this particular regard.

The aspect that she wasn't happy with was that they became increasingly secretive. Where they used to openly talk about what they did and even bring it to her attention, now they were much more reluctant to do so. They were also less eager to talk about it once it came into the open, preferring to look down and keep quiet, or mumble inaudibly when pressed to respond.

On a couple of occasions, she also caught them acting in their old ways, the ways that she thought she had disciplined out of them. She noticed that they only behaved this way when they thought they wouldn't be found out. This made her wonder how effective her approach to child rearing had been, seeing that it had not produced the desired effect but only an appearance of that, while producing another effect that she did not approve of or intend.

The easiest way to come to terms with this kind of failure is to redefine it. We can observe that, when we perform an action and fail to get the desired result, we have effectively expanded our knowledge of the consequences of this particular action that we have lacked before. This outcome is clearly useful to us. To interpret it as a failure would be to shun the tangible benefits that it has to offer.[12]

A failure truly occurs only when we have gained no benefit from the experience – when we have both failed to produce the desired result and failed to learn from not doing so. Such an outcome is tragic. Fortunately, avoiding it is entirely within our control. How much we learn from our experience will depend on the relevant skills, but not whether we learn anything at all. The experience will have something to teach us even if we are grappling with these concepts for the very first time.

Choosing Unworthy Goals

This is the last kind of failure, which occurs when we accomplish a task and watch it produce the desired effect, only to realize that the effect was far less desirable than we hoped it would be.

---

[12] This never-say-die attitude is epitomised by the words of the famous inventor Thomas Alva Edison: "I haven't failed. I've found 10,000 ways that don't work."

It might seem odd that this should happen with any frequency. Surely accomplishing our goals is the very definition of success. At the highest level, this is indeed the case. As far as I can tell, the desire for happiness is our underlying motivation, the overarching goal that sponsors all our other goals. We can't go wrong by achieving it. However, this goal is much too broad to lend itself to practical application. We need to set more specific goals that we can tie to concrete situations that lead directly to their realization. It is these specific goals that can be misconstrued.

This is the kind of failure that is most frequently associated with life crises. Because it can take years and even decades to reach the main goals in life, should we then discover that these goals weren't worthy of their stature, we could well become profoundly disillusioned.

EXAMPLE:

As a highly influential investment banker, Harold was the epitome of success. His flourishing career in the financial industry has enabled him to live in a spacious house and drive a luxury car. His wife didn't need to work and instead devoted much of her time to taking care of their son. All of their material needs and most desires were comfortably met.

Beneath that idyllic surface, Harold was unfulfilled. He had lived the material dream and found that something was missing. He couldn't quite put his finger on what it was. He just knew that a person with his accomplishments should have felt deeply satisfied, which he didn't.

He did feel good about his successful career, a position that gave him a great deal of power and prestige, and an income that left very few things out of his reach. It was other aspects of his life that he was having difficulty with. Working most evenings and weekends left him with precious little time to spend with his wife and son, not to mention his extended family and friends outside of work. His hobbies had also fallen by the wayside. He had the desire, the money, and the knowledge to accomplish a great deal outside of his career, but no time to do it in.

The way forward was clear. If he was not satisfied with his current accomplishments, it was because he hadn't progressed far enough. He had to climb further up the corporate ladder to get a more gratifying taste of success. He knew that he had the talent to do that, even make a name for himself in the international arena, but his determination was starting to falter. He was beginning to see through the propaganda and realize what this approach to life had to offer him. It was only more and more of what he already had in abundance, and less and less of what he already lacked. Something didn't add up here. Somehow the whole scheme had gone wrong. Having largely reached his life goals, he stood there looking back and wondering what it was all for.

In theory at least, this is not all that different from misunderstanding cause and effect. Rather than failing to anticipate how actions and goals tie together, we fail to grasp how specific goals come together to bring about more general ones. The solution that presents itself is also similar. By observing that experiencing these undesirable consequences has enabled us to correct our misperception of them, we can appreciate the opportunity to expand our knowledge base that this has presented us with.

In practice, however, discovering that the direction that our lives have gone in is faulty can be devastating. It is not so much a case of questioning our abilities as of wondering why we should bother applying them, since even utilizing them to their full potential is no guarantee of success.

Mastering Failure

It should be apparent by now that the challenges that failure presents us with are not troublesome at all when looked at through the lens of rationality. Even the discovery that we've spent our whole lives going in a wrong direction can be remedied by a simple application of the tools given in this book, such as observing other people to uncover a more worthwhile way to live and paying close attention to our feelings when evaluating alternative approaches.

The challenges of genuine failure are, largely, and of failure in perception, completely, emotional in nature. The danger that they pose is one of derailing the process of deliberate living, not because we've found that it doesn't work, but because we cannot bring ourselves to apply it.

If we are to overcome profound disillusionment with the way we have lived, we need one essential insight. This is that the life crisis that arises from it is an expression of our past, not our future. If we allow ourselves to get stuck in the acute regret that we may feel for the bad decisions that we've made, it can rob us of the opportunity to turn our lives around. Like guilt, it only has the power that we give it.

Mastering failure basically amounts to curbing the emotional ravages that it can cause within us. The previous sections mentioned some of the means that we have at our disposal. What remains to be done is to use these tools whenever the opportunity presents itself, thereby developing the necessary skills. Ideally, we would like these skills to be in good shape whenever failure strikes. Like any skill, however, our proficiency with them grows with use.

This seems obvious enough, so much so that it shouldn't warrant any special consideration. Unfortunately, experiencing failure is a decidedly distasteful event in our lives. Even if we succeed at redefining it in more positive terms, it is still likely to stir some unpleasant emotions. These give us reason enough to avoid it, thereby preventing us from developing the skills with which to combat failure.

Increasing the incidence of failure in our lives is not the answer. Failing exams, losing our job and other such incidents are a high price to pay just so that we can learn to get to grips with the negative emotions that they sponsor. What we need is a way to simulate the emotional consequences of failure, but without the accompanying negative effects. In other words, we need to master failure in a virtual setting.

This environment has been provided by many games and plays that our society has traditionally engaged in. All we had to do was to become emotionally attached to the proceedings, and the failure to achieve our goals would become hard to distinguish from the real thing. With the advent of video games, the repertoire of ways in which we can simulate real-life conditions has grown tremendously. We can put these products of human ingenuity to very fruitful use in helping us hone the skills with which to combat failure when it really does take place.

EXAMPLE:

Marvin's home computer was a big part of his life. Whenever he was tired from work, feeling down, or worn out from having to deal with all kinds of problems, he would start up his favorite game and be instantly transported to another world, one that faithfully dovetailed with his imagination. There, he would get to live his fantasies as the king, the chief architect, or the commander of vast armies. The experience was immensely satisfying.

Occasionally, he would overreach himself. His armies would get annihilated, or the inhabitants of his city would get fed up with his handling of their affairs and would pack up and leave. What was intended to be an energizing triumph would turn into a depressing failure. This was the worst – when his escape from reality proved to be no different from it.

Until it occurred to him that the only consequences of failure at computer games were psychological. None of it mattered beyond what he allowed it to. It's not as if trolls would come and haunt him at his work if he failed to contain their bloodthirstiness in the game. This thought led to another. If the environment of computer games was so rich as to allow him to completely immerse himself in it, yet nevertheless virtual, why not use it to help him get to grips with failure?

He loaded one of his favorite games. This time, he set the level of difficulty high enough not to be able to withstand his enemies, but low enough to sustain a glimmer of hope that he just might prevail. He soon got lost in the game, drawing on all of his skill and resourcefulness to neutralize the threat of alien invasion, only to find his efforts come to naught. It was devastating. Only this time, instead of angrily throwing away the gamepad and cursing and sulking over the loss, he decided to face it.

He realized that he was heavily emotionally invested in the outcome of the game. If he were to be able to cope with loss, he would have to decrease the importance that he attached to winning. With practice, he came to appreciate the beauty of the game without it hinging on its conclusion. He even started taking himself less seriously. He learned how to pause and reflect and take stock of the situation while in the midst of emotional turmoil. It wasn't long before he was laughing at his foibles.

Overcoming negative emotional effects of failure is a landmark achievement. When contending with genuine failure, it enables us to focus strictly on the problem itself and shed the emotional burden that would otherwise weigh us down.

With perceptive failure, it literally removes this impediment from our way, leaving nothing to hold us back from trying out new things in order to learn and grow. Life becomes an adventure that we cannot fail at. Progress is assured, no matter which path we take. All that we need to do is pay attention while we are on it.

Perhaps the most important insight regarding failure in perception is that it is not the end. It might feel like the end when, after a long while, our goals remain beyond our reach, or when we reach them only to realize that they are not what they were cracked up to be. With an extensive set of well-honed tools at our side, we can react to these developments in strictly constructive ways, taking them in our stride and using them to fashion our lives into something even better than what they used to be. To a large extent, it is the subsequent taste of success that enables us to redefine failure in strictly positive terms, and even appreciate learning the many valuable lessons that it had to teach us.

Summary: Questions to Ask Myself

What actions do I perform in an effort to achieve certain external results? What actions do I perform simply as an expression of who I am? What effect do these different actions have on me?

What have I failed at? How can I redefine these incidences of failure in positive terms?

How can I practice dealing with emotional effects of failure?

How would I live my life if I knew that I couldn't fail?

Part 3:
What Are the Effects of Living Deliberately?

The Difficulty of Pursuing Deliberate Living

"Courage is not the absence of fear, but rather the judgment that something else is more important than fear."

Ambrose Redmoon

Part two of the book has highlighted various difficulties that we may encounter when attempting to live deliberately. Formulating worthwhile goals, understanding cause and effect, evaluating the consequences of our actions, and many other aspects of the process all present their unique challenges that have to be overcome if we are to master this approach to living. All of these challenges stem from lack of knowledge. As we contemplate, observe and gain experience, we gradually accumulate the knowledge with which to surmount them.

These are not the only challenges that we will face, however. There is an entirely different class of challenges that emerge once the necessary knowledge has been attained. They test not our ability to find the best course of action, but our resolve, our strength of conviction to walk down the path that we know we should.

These challenges are more personal in nature than those already discussed. Which ones come to the fore strongly depends on one's background. I will list those that featured the most prominently for me in the hope that at least some people can relate to them and find value in their discussion.

Going It Alone

I was raised in a Christian family and remained a Christian until the age of 29. Most members of my immediate and extended family were likewise Christian. We used the Church's teachings as a framework within which to construct our personal belief systems. We may have differed in the details, but disagreements were usually about nothing more than the extent to which various teachings should be adopted, the ideal being to embrace them fully.

Leaving the Church has left me without this support structure. The dilemmas suddenly extended well beyond finding ways to accept a preordained list of tenets. I had to decide where to get those tenets from, to what extent to rely on external guidelines as opposed to my own thoughts, feelings and experience, and even whether my own thoughts really stemmed from me, or were merely unconsciously internalized from some other source.

An easy way out would have been to replace the authority of the Church with some other authority – another religion, or perhaps the scientific establishment. Instead, I decided to go my own way. This has left me without an organization to belong to from which I could derive a sense of identity.

Such a situation definitely has its good points. Not giving my allegiance to an external authority has made me less susceptible to manipulation. I'm also not dependent on it for a sense of identity, where criticism of the organization can be perceived as an attack on who I am. Lastly, no organization can supply us with a complete set of guidelines on how to live our lives. We have no choice but to derive some for ourselves. Walking one's own path explicitly acknowledges this fact.

With time, I've arrived at the conclusion that it doesn't make sense to come together with a group of like-minded individuals in search of identity, regardless of who the individuals are and how closely their thinking mirrors ours. Who we are is personal and unique. It cannot be arrived at through any kind of inter-personal agreement. Where coming together makes sense instead is to assist us on our search, as well as to help us express the identity that is the fruit of that search.

Still, if one is used to deriving one's identity from an organization, dispensing with the very idea can be hard. It leads to a crisis of identity; where the fundamentals of how we relate to the world we live in begin to shift. Because we depend on these fundamentals to frame our conduct, we are left without effective guidance while they are in flux. With time, they take root again, hopefully pointing us in a more desirable direction from there on.

After the change in direction is completed, the challenge of going it alone consists of continuing with the practices that have given rise to it and unearthing the many hidden assumptions that still underpin our beliefs and thereby our conduct. The idea is to distinguish essential from redundant assumptions, and purposefully choose the former while dispensing with the latter.

Due to the conformist nature of our society, there is an additional challenge in the form of pressure to adhere to social norms that is exerted by the majority of people who have not made such a change. It is not easy for them to understand why I have no desire to support the home team or proclaim my nationality. Because they still derive their sense of identity from these organizations, not partaking in them borders on an insult. It takes a great deal of care to avoid provoking defensive reactions while standing firm in one's rejection of membership.

Fear of Crises

The chapter <u>When Things Fall Apart</u> alluded to the relatively high incidence of challenging developments that characterize deliberate living. This might appear counterintuitive at first. Isn't this approach to living supposed to make life work better?

In my experience, deliberate living does lead to substantial improvement in the handling of various situations. In many cases, where I used to make the same error on numerous occasions, I have been able to adjust my attitude and behavior so that the negative consequences were lessened or eliminated altogether. To accomplish this, I've had to examine my behavior and bring under the spotlight the beliefs that gave rise to it.

The process of introspection that is needed to accomplish such changes can be intimidating. The unease stems from its unpredictable nature. The risk of subjecting my views to scrutiny was that I might be forced to dispense with beliefs that I have come to rely upon for guidance. When this did occur, watching a favored belief brought into question was unnerving.

This has happened in a wide variety of situations, but none more frequently than in my relationship with my immediate family. Time and again, I've had to acknowledge that my idea of how my relationship with my wife should work wasn't as sound as I had previously thought, and that, even after years of careful scrutiny, it still lay at the root of some of our problems. Interaction with my children has made it very clear to me that I wasn't adequately prepared for raising them, and that I needed to question many of the commonly held assumptions that had served as the foundation of our relationship.

When a belief under scrutiny plays a foundational role in one's worldview, bringing it into question leads to a crisis. Leaving Christianity behind was one such crisis for me – it made me question and discard many of the assumptions that formed the basis of my worldview. Failing at my electrical engineering studies was another – it made me question my own ability to choose a direction in life and see it through.

We can expect upheavals of our belief structure to be a relatively frequent companion if we want to progress in the manner in which we relate to the world around us. They are an unavoidable part of the process of change. The old beliefs have to dissipate to make it possible for us to assimilate the new. Hindsight makes it clear that the long-term benefits of this outweigh the short-term costs many times over. However, if we are facing a prospect of uneasy change or are caught in the midst of it, the challenge can be daunting.

Fear of the Future

There are several facets to existence in the modern world that have to be mastered if one is to succeed at it. The first one has to do with our ability to acquire sustenance, which translates to earning an income. Due to the competitive nature of our society, this typically involves a substantial investment of time and effort in acquiring quality education and furthering our career. The danger of not doing this is that we will become uncompetitive, which will directly bring our ability to earn sufficient income into question.

The second facet arises from recognizing the limitations of the first. We won't always be able to earn an income. With time, we will grow too old to work productively. We also face the risk of becoming incapacitated due to injury or illness. Furthermore, some of the risks that we face – such as causing a multiple-car accident or having our house burn down – extend beyond our ability to cover even when in our prime. We therefore need to plan for these eventualities and mitigate the risks by investing in various forms of insurance and retirement planning.

Unfortunately, these risk-mitigation strategies don't take us far enough. The world is a volatile place. We also need to follow the news and watch trends so that we can be prepared to deal with economic crises and, depending on where we live, political, military and ecological crises as well. It was this kind of awareness that had enabled my family to get out of Yugoslavia a year before the civil war broke out, and my wife's family to leave Zimbabwe before it deteriorated under Robert Mugabe's rule.

Keeping abreast of all of these developments is sufficiently challenging to engage us for the duration of our lives. Playing by the rules of our society, as outlined above, can be so demanding that it leaves us with insufficient time and energy to examine those rules to see whether and how we might want to change them.

This has created a problem for me because I have come to reject much of the "wisdom" that is proclaimed by the modern lifestyle. There is no doubt left in my mind that it should be rejected. We can do far better, both as individuals and as a society, than, for example, striving to maximize material gain and social status, or minimizing our interdependence by hiding behind regulations and relying on insurance and retirement planning.

Still, the system that I'm trying to change is the present-day reality. Like it or not, my physical survival and wellbeing derive from my ability to play by its rules. The problem is compounded by my family's dependence on the same. As much as I may resent the limitations that it imposes, I can only ignore them at our peril.

This leaves me with a fine balancing act to follow – making a sufficient investment in our physical wellbeing so that it is not likely to be brought into question, while sparing enough to dedicate to bringing about the much needed personal and social change. The desire for life fulfillment leaves no doubt for me that a substantial investment in personal and social transformation needs to be made. However, from the perspective of personal security, such a course of action can be unnerving.

Frustration, Sadness, and Despair

The story of success detailed in part two of this book is shadowed by a dark twin – a story of frustration, sadness, and despair. As I started applying the principles of deliberate living and saw them work, I've come to realize that these tools are available to us all. There is nothing that precludes every person from making use of them, even if mastering them does require a great deal of dedication.

I've also come to realize that many people, perhaps the majority, are not willing to take this step. They are enthralled with the dramas that permeate their lives, even if these are accompanied by suffering. They interpret the circumstances in their lives in a decidedly unpleasant manner, cast themselves in the role of a victim of those circumstances, and then openly lament their misfortune.

While I shared these sentiments, I could sympathize with their plight, feel sorry for the bad turn of events, and help them change the circumstances that have caused them distress. Mending the circumstances invariably proved to be too ambitious an undertaking since nothing less than perfection would do – any kind of failure anywhere could lead to the perception of being victimized and so trigger the dramatic response. Nevertheless, simply understanding what the people were going through and approving of their handling of the matter was usually enough.

Having successfully eliminated most of the drama from my life, in many cases by changing my perception of circumstances rather than the circumstances themselves, I've gradually formed a different picture of the above behavior. It has become increasingly difficult to relate to it. The hardest part is that the people typically don't want to resolve the matter, even though they are obviously in distress and keep asking for help. What they are actually looking for is sympathy and continuance of the same behavior. I've had to focus on seeing the humor in the situation in an effort to curb the frustration that would otherwise result.

On a larger scale, we have reached a point in the development of our society where very few of the problems that afflict us are beyond our control. Thanks to tremendous improvements in communication and transportation in the recent centuries and especially decades, we have the means to identify the problems that afflict us – epidemics, natural disasters, malnutrition, poverty, illiteracy, and a whole host of others – in any part of the globe, and mobilize the resources necessary to remedy them.

We have done this to some extent – practically eliminated illiteracy in the developed world, summoned international aid to assist with the recovery from natural disasters, established a global network of voluntary blood donation services, created a diverse array of free computer software, and many other success stories. Despite these efforts, I think it would be fair to say that the society that we have created is a pitiful shadow of what it would be if each one of us realized his or her full potential.

It could be argued that creating a utopian society or one close to it lies beyond our capabilities. The dilemmas posed by large-scale social interaction amidst great diversity of beliefs and preferences are certainly complex and formidable. Resolving them to widespread satisfaction could well lie beyond our reach. However, I'm inclined to think that, taken collectively, rather than failing at the challenge of creating a society that works for everyone, we have by and large not even attempted it. Most of the effort is instead directed towards maintaining the society in its present form, where one has to confront this momentum if social improvements are to be conceded.

The consequences of this state of affairs are dire. I can see them around me practically every day. Swathes of people are struggling with the challenge of basic survival, with many failing at it. Large segments of society are denigrated by the economic system that doesn't need them, their dignity and integrity sacrificed to state handouts, begging, and crime. Those fortunate enough to be employed often struggle to find fulfillment in their work.

Probing beyond direct human concerns, we can see that plants and animals are exploited with callous disregard for any qualities that they may have save those that make them immediately useful to us; many have been driven to or tether on the edge of extinction. In fact, the environment as a whole is often seen as nothing more than a resource base for us to consume and a dumping ground for the countless toxins that we produce.

If the problems that I'm describing don't appear this way to us, it may be because we have grown accustomed to them and accept them as an integral part of life, much as our ancestors accepted slavery, denigration of women, serfdom and perpetual warfare as the way the world worked that could not be changed. Looking at these past social traits now is not too dissimilar to looking at our present society from the perspective of a near-utopian one. It is not easy to see humor in this situation, considering the widespread suffering that it brings to large segments of humanity and other creatures with whom we share this planet; suffering that, given the choice, I'm sure they would prefer to avoid.

This betrays another motivation that I have for writing this book. I don't think that we can overcome the countless problems that we face by inventing a new political or economic system. We can pass legislation to deal with the symptoms of our problems, but their cause runs much deeper. It rests with who we perceive ourselves to be, and how we relate to ourselves, other people, and the world around us. The ability to overcome these problems depends on our capacity to reinvent not our social structures, but ourselves.

According to most researchers in the field of psychology, conformist consciousness is the most common form of consciousness found in our society. This is a cause for concern. Reinventing ourselves with urgency and purpose is an impossible task if we are in the habit of conforming to social norms.

I have written this book with the aim to accelerate and sustain the prerequisite inner transformation. It is my hope that this will in turn trigger the much-needed social transformation grounded in genuine preference for a sustainable lifestyle that works for everyone. This is what is needed to tackle the underlying causes of our problems instead of merely their symptoms and to put solutions in place that will endure.

We can envisage a far grander reality than the one that we have created for ourselves here today. The only obstacle that stands in the way of putting this vision into practice is our conformance to society in its present form and the resulting habitual maintenance of the status quo.

Summary: Questions to Ask Myself

From where do I derive my sense of identity?

How do I balance living by the rules of the society with examining those rules and trying to change them?

How far am I prepared to pursue the social implications of deliberate living?

The Value of Attaining Deliberate Living

"Let the beauty of what you love be what you do."
                                                    Jelalludin Rumi

In addition to pointing out difficulties, part two of this book has also exposed some of the benefits that may be brought about through this way of living. Some are implicit in the main text, while others are revealed through examples.

The purpose of this chapter is to emphasize the foremost benefits of deliberate living, in case they have not been clearly conveyed, or their importance not sufficiently highlighted. Looking back, these are the changes that feature the most prominently in my memories. They effectively play the role of ambassadors for this way of living – they tend to draw the attention of people who are attracted to deliberate living, but might not have been aware of it and haven't actively pursued it yet.

The sections contained in this chapter are not really separate entities that coexist independently of one another. They are mutually reinforcing. The growth that we undergo is likely to manifest in several different areas, if not all of them. It is only broken down into separate sections for ease of presentation.

Not Getting Hurt

I have listed this first because I believe it to be absolutely critical to unlocking most of the other benefits that are associated with deliberate living. As was explained in the section Experiencing Pain, pain limits our choices. Whenever we find ourselves to be hurt, we would do well to seek healing before formulating a response to the circumstances that have left us in distress; otherwise we may well regret our reaction later on, when the pain of the event has subsided.

The approach to living described in this book is effective at preventing the hurt from ever taking place. To begin with, consciously choosing words and actions, and hopefully thoughts, feelings and beliefs as well enables us to decide on the role that they play in our lives. We have chosen them, manifested them, experienced them, and probably caused others to do the same, but they are not who we are intrinsically. As a result, we have the ability to detach ourselves from them when it is appropriate to do so. We can change them without undermining our identity in the process, and so are not compelled to feel personally attacked when they are criticized.

The process of detachment is eased by not carrying the burden of past judgments into the present. This enables us to critically examine our conduct on regular basis in an effort to improve upon it. Frequent introspection accompanied with lack of self-condemnation allows us to peer deeply into events that would otherwise be too painful to look at, and see them in ways that cause them to unravel. It is also able to accept other people's criticism in a constructive manner, even when this is not the spirit in which it was offered.

Acquiring this level of knowledge and acceptance of ourselves has a side effect of giving us a sense of security. This sense is further bolstered by grasping just how much of the world that we live in is built on pretence, and how difficult it is to find security in what we know to be a fabrication.

For example, not so long ago, someone I know had chosen to speak in a less-than-flattering manner about my deceased father. Not only were the accusations disrespectful, but unfounded as well. I have very fond memories of my father. It goes without saying that he has committed his share of mistakes, but even so, I have the greatest respect for the kind of life that he has lived. Regardless, it is hardly appropriate to attack someone who is no longer around to defend himself.

It is precisely because of the sense of security that I derive from my acceptance of who my father was, with all his virtues and flaws, that I felt no need to defend him from this person's attack. Nothing she said could threaten my memories of him or cause me to look at him in an unfavorable light. This made it possible for me to shift my attention away from the object of her attack to her motivation for it. I realized that she must have been hurting in some way to say the things that she did, and that the best response was compassion rather than retaliation.

Release of Judgment

Release of judgment follows from not self-identifying with one's behavior, as mentioned in the previous section. It might not be clear what the term *judgment* means in this context or what it means to release it, so I will illustrate the meaning with an example.

Say that a person engages in conduct that draws widespread criticism from his peers. If he doesn't self-identify with his behavior, that is, if he perceives a distinction between who he is *now* and what he has done *in the past*, then he will not feel personally threatened by the criticism and will be able to use it to evaluate his conduct to reach conclusions about it. However, if he doesn't perceive that distinction, he will interpret the criticism as a personal attack. Instead of using the criticism to his advantage to learn and grow, he will attempt to defend himself from it.

Consciously or unconsciously, the person evaluates the feedback that he receives from the environment from the perspective of survival – screening for anything that might endanger it – and sets up a defense against it when he perceives it as a threat. It is not even necessary for criticism to take place. If defense is vigilant enough, it will treat observations as criticisms and mount resistance to them. As a result, even when people merely state what they've observed and do so disinterestedly or with the best intentions, they can provoke a defensive response. It is this binary interpretation of sensory input as either threatening or not that I'm referring to as *judgment*.

I'm calling it judgment to distinguish it from conclusions based on evaluation. Evaluation grapples with the content of criticism in an attempt to reach conclusions about it. Judgment of this nature instead entails a change of focus from the criticism to its source, and a shift away from understanding to neutralizing it.

Examples are frighteningly widespread. My own behavior was riddled with them until not so long ago. One of my most alert defenses was in the area of my work and was organized around the knowledge of various computer technologies, which I knew I wasn't sufficiently proficient in. It took me many years to acknowledge and accept this state of affairs, and stop deflecting my co-workers' probes that I feared might expose the deficiency.

Judgment, as described here, is a major hindrance to growth. It strives to identify and eliminate threats to our current way of living. Because growth amounts to change, it poses a threat by its very nature. Looking at life through the lens of judgment, we are unable to even ascertain where we stand, let alone find ways to improve it. Judgment arrests the growth process at the very beginning.

Once mastered, the ability to dispense with unsolicited judgment can be extended to other people as well. Just as we can peer deeply into our past conduct to see it for what it is instead of looking the other way, we can do the same with the conduct of other people. Just as we can focus our energy on making an accurate statement of who we are next time we act instead of berating ourselves for our last failed attempt, we can extend the same courtesy to others.

The implications of this are far-reaching. We can look behind another person's conduct to uncover the beliefs and the circumstances that have sponsored it, even if we don't agree with her behavior and may consider it immoral. We can work at empathizing with and understanding where another person is coming from even as we are the target of his wrath. We can do these things even if their intention is to hurt us.

With the need to judge out of the way, we literally become free to engage in whatever response is the most beneficial in any given circumstances. I have found that the move away from judging and towards examination, understanding, and empathy greatly enhances these skills. It also has an empowering effect on the people on whom it is applied.

Being able to identify a defensive reaction and grasp its underlying motivation makes it far easier to interact with people when they operate in this mode. It leaves no doubt that the only way forward is to first address the need for the judgmental interpretation. Only once they feel secure in their position are they able to accept penetrating observations of their conduct, and respond to them in a constructive manner.

Furthermore, many of those I've met carry a burden of guilt around with them, though it may be necessary to get to know them before this becomes apparent. It is a combination of self-judgment and the fear of being judged by others that keeps their burden in place. Helping them offload it no matter what may have caused it has been as beneficial for them as it has been rewarding for me.

Conscious Evolution

This was hinted at in the previous section. It follows directly from turning one's focus away from judging every action as right or wrong and towards dissecting it for better understanding and improved personal application. With time, conscious evolution becomes the defining characteristic of deliberate living.

To begin with, it seems quite obvious to me that, as individual human beings, we are gradually evolving. While there may be exceptions, the people I know have generally grown wiser as they have gotten older and acquired more life experience. This doesn't mean that older people are necessarily wiser than younger ones, but that a particular individual acquires insights on her life journey that she gradually weaves into her worldview, and so becomes wiser as she grows older.

The effect that deliberate living has on this gradual process of positive change is that it no longer proceeds by happenstance. No longer is growth an accidental by-product of difficult circumstances or fortuitous encounters with future role models. It becomes something that is consciously sought and intentionally directed. Rather than being driven by environmental changes, it is now driven internally, by one's own will.

Every situation that we encounter presents us with an opportunity to define ourselves relative to it. Doing so consciously can be immensely rewarding; in a way, the practice feeds on its own success. Coming up with and demonstrating a worthwhile self-definition in a given situation generates desirable experience, which stimulates the search for even more worthy self-perceptions and means of realizing them, whose application in turn yields even more profound experiences. From my present perspective, it looks like an endless upward spiral, with each step being more rewarding than those that preceded it.

It is difficult to watch from a distance and appreciate the full extent that this change in approach has on the living of one's life. I didn't appreciate it until sometime after I found myself on the same journey. Outwardly it appears much the same except that the person's outlook is noticeably more positive and contented. Inwardly, however, it is like a difference between sleepwalking and moving forward with purpose and confidence. Doing so might make what came before not appear like living at all.

Transcendence of Rules and Regulations

Acting as one's own highest authority is decidedly at odds with living in a society that prizes adherence to its rules and regulations. Viewed from the perspective of legal consequences, unethically following rules is preferable to ethically contravening them. When those rules are taken away from us – during a breakdown in law enforcement, for example – many of us struggle to decide how to conduct ourselves.

It should be obvious that formulating and enforcing rules is severely limited in what it can accomplish. Numerous objections can be raised. For instance, rules are much more general than the situations in which they are applied, so they easily miss important details. They also cannot be utilized constructively without the aid of the relevant life experience. And they do nothing to address the desire to do harm, which is the underlying cause of the problems that they are trying to solve.

The very existence of rules confuses the issue. Considering the large number of rules present in our society, it is all too easy to conclude that this is what defines how we should live our lives, and that behavior is acceptable so long as it doesn't break any of the rules. If we want our society to work, however, we simply have no alternative but to master taking personal responsibility for our conduct. Formulating and enforcing rules can help us until sufficient growth is attained, but it cannot be our primary goal.

EXAMPLE:

A popular way of using rules to increase road safety is to impose a speed limit – the maximum speed that a vehicle is

The Value of Attaining Deliberate Living

allowed to travel at on the designated stretch of road. Failure to adhere to this limit typically attracts the penalty of a fine. If the speed limit is grossly exceeded, more stringent measures can be taken. If we break the speed limit and cause an accident, we will have a better understanding of why it was instituted in the first place.

This might give us the impression that the speed at which we drive is appropriate as long as it does not exceed the speed limit. This is not the case, however. The appropriate speed is heavily dependent on circumstances. On a deserted road on a clear day, it might be overly restrictive. In the presence of rain, mist, ice on the road, blind side roads, traffic congestion, small children, etc, it might not be restrictive enough. If we want to ensure that the speed that we drive at is always appropriate, we have no choice but to discover how the various factors influence it, and learn to recognize them when we see them. Instituting a fixed speed limit is simply no substitute.

Deliberate living provides us with the means of transcending rules and regulations. By transcending, I mean rendering them unnecessary. This might sound like a utopian ideal, but I seriously think that it is potentially much closer than we realize. The reason is that it doesn't require us to master deliberate living in all its nuances; becoming engaged in the process is all it will take. This is no small commitment, especially considering that, in many ways, our society actively discourages it. However, turning this around is well within our capabilities.

Once we set our mind to learning and growth, punishing us for the errors that we make, as rules currently require, becomes counterproductive. This approach is only effective for people who have no desire to learn from their mistakes. Others are much better served by assistance on their journey. If someone has not yet made concrete steps towards living authentically, we are better off helping them engage in the process than punishing them for not having done so.

With punishment removed from the picture, rules stop being rules and become merely guidelines. They are still useful to us in this form. The insights encapsulated in them still illuminate our way. In so doing, they now enhance our ability to live deliberately instead of working against it.

The Basis of Morality

Of all the questions that we tend to grapple with on daily basis, I find those that pertain to morality among the most perplexing. Sure, some of them are obvious. We easily conclude that murder is immoral, even if we may need a bit of time to come up with a satisfactory justification for that conclusion. But is the death penalty immoral? Here the public opinion is divided. Its practice has its adherents and detractors. Both are able to marshal considerable arguments in support of their position. From my involvement in such discussions, I've come to realize that this has a lot to do with the nebulous nature of the concept of morality. When we say that something is moral, what do we mean by that?

The question can be particularly challenging for those of us who don't live by a fixed set of rules, but evaluate each circumstance to select a preferred course of action. Even if we do live by a fixed code, however, it is impossibly unlikely that this code will contain a clear guideline for every scenario that we can encounter in our lives. Some interpolation and interpretation of the rules will still be required.

The process presented in this book can be used to shed some light on the question of morality. From this perspective, behavior is moral if it helps us achieve our goals, and goals are moral if their fulfillment gives rise to desirable emotions. This gives us a basis for our concept of morality, or alternatively, enables us to dispense with it altogether. The value of this approach is in being methodical. It enables us to derive an answer in an unfamiliar situation and refine that answer as new knowledge comes to light, especially as it is further verified through experience. The answer obtained in this manner is one that we can agree with and understand why we have adopted it.

EXAMPLE:

Many arguments can be given in justification of the death penalty, particularly when dealing with a convicted murderer. Some of them recognize that the murderer has prejudiced himself by his criminal act and deserves to endure the same harsh treatment that he has subjected his victims to, especially as a means of compensating the victim's family. Others point to the financial cost and callousness of the alternative punishment of life imprisonment. Still others advocate it as a deterrent against future crimes.

Many arguments can also be given against the death penalty. Some recognize the inherent value of human life, even that of a hardened criminal. Others point to the ineffectiveness of the death penalty at reducing the incidence of crime. Still others are irked by the hypocrisy of resorting to state-sanctioned murder to demonstrate that murder will not be tolerated by the law.

When viewed from the perspective of the process described in this book, we see that the question of the death penalty's morality is not centered on what the criminal or the victim has done or deserved, but on who we are in relation to that.

One way of doing this is to begin by deciding on our goals. What is it that we wish to accomplish in this context – what kind of experience do we wish to have? Do we wish to experience ourselves as compassionate – compassionate without bound or only towards the victim's family and friends? Do we wish to experience living in a just society, and can we distinguish between justice and revenge? Do we wish to hurt or do we wish to heal?

Once we have decided on our goals, we can then evaluate the practice of the death penalty to see whether it helps us achieve them. If not, we can conclude that it is dysfunctional (immoral) and look for an alternative. If it does, we can bring our goals back under the spotlight to see whether they were worthwhile or whether we should choose again.

An alternative approach is simply to go through with the death penalty – by being present as it is administered, for example – and pay attention to the resulting experience. Then we can evaluate the experience to decide whether it was desirable.

Summary: Questions to Ask Myself

How do I avoid getting hurt?

How do I avoid responding judgmentally?

The Value of Attaining Deliberate Living

Regarding social norms:
Which rules of my society, religion, or culture do I disagree with?
Why do I disagree with them?
What conduct do I consider to be superior?

Regarding morality:
What makes an action moral or immoral?
Does the concept of morality apply to intentions?

Likely Criticism

"A man or a woman recognizes God and starts out. The others say he or she is losing faith."

Jelalludin Rumi

Part one has dealt with some of the criticisms that are often leveled at the life philosophy that forms the foundation of deliberate living as outlined in this book. This chapter in turn examines the criticism that our behavior is likely to attract as we put those concepts into practice.

While many people can appreciate the positive changes brought on by deliberate living – especially those described in the previous chapter – when they see them in others, some respond quite negatively to them. Of the reactions that I've seen, most seem to be sponsored by either fear or resentment.

A fearful reaction results from being faced with a way of life that is radically different from what one is familiar and comfortable with, and feeling threatened by it. It is a defensive reaction that sometimes manifests as aggression. In a way, it amounts to a tacit recognition that deliberate living is a force to be reckoned with, but instead of wielding it for one's benefit, one seeks to eliminate it.

A resentful reaction likewise results from confronting an alien way of life. Instead of stomping on it, one exalts it to such an extent that it ends up being placed out of one's reach. This leads to resentment, which is essentially a demand to remove it from one's sight as it is simply cruel to parade something so worthwhile yet unattainable in one's presence.

Like the resolve-based challenges of achieving deliberate living, the criticism is highly personal in nature. Instead of depending on one's background, it depends on the belief system and the state of being of those whom one comes into contact with. I will again mention those that featured the most prominently in my life, with the same motivation as before.

Excessive Change

Of all the criticisms of deliberate living that I've come across, this one cuts to the core of it more than any other. It bypasses the considerations of how desirable the end product is to attack the very notion of change itself.

To appreciate the criticism, it has to be understood that living authentically is largely at odds with the modern society. I discarded many of the fundamental values and beliefs that I was raised with shortly after embarking on this journey. They simply didn't fit me. As a result, I started thinking differently and reacting differently to many of the same situations.

Ongoing change presented considerable difficulties for people who associated with me. They had to drop their old ideas, borne of experience, of how I perceive the world and react to it to discover what these had morphed into in the recent past. It made our association less predictable, and so more difficult to depend on.

This difficulty was felt most acutely in intimate relationships, particularly with that of my wife. Leaving behind the church that I had attended regularly would have been shock enough; coupled with a de-prioritization of my career and a looming change of direction, radically different views on marriage and parenting, a dietary change from a meat-eating to a Jain diet, and a whole host of other adjustments that unfolded in the space of several years, it placed tremendous strain on our relationship. She had to get to know me again, and keep getting to know me, just to be able to relate to me.

This is a lot to expect from other people. They didn't ask for the change, so in a way, it is unfair to subject them to it. Of course, it is unrealistic to expect people to remain the same for the remainder of their lives. It is the rate and sheer size of the change, where the very fundamentals of one's outlook are brought into question, which pose a problem.

On the other hand, retaining dysfunctional views for the convenience of other people is simply unworkable. The only way forward that I can see is to remain true to myself, with all the chipping away of social masks and false views that this entails, while exposing other people to them as gently as I can and with as few demands and expectations as I can.

Lack of Emotions

This particular criticism is surprisingly likely. I say surprisingly because this whole approach to living is rooted in emotions. To say that deliberate living results in a lack of emotions is decidedly at odds with what this approach to living is all about.

A different interpretation of this criticism, whereby deliberate living results in a lack of outward display of the emotions that the person is feeling, is also inaccurate. There is nothing about the process described in this book that urges us to refrain from openly displaying our emotions. Where is the criticism coming from, then?

A look at the situations in which this criticism is typically leveled can help provide the answer. I usually see it happen in situations that are emotionally charged, to which participants react strongly and with little or no control. Because they perceive themselves to be at the mercy of their own powerful experience, they expect everyone else to react the same way. If they don't, they are described as lacking emotions, or at least the particular emotions that they were expected to display. This is seen as a more plausible explanation than that these emotions were present in a person, but that the person was able to voluntarily select other emotions – through a change in focus and engaging in appropriate sponsoring action – that he instead wished to experience.

Lack of Accountability for Mistakes

A prominent feature of this approach to living is a decisive move away from judging people and apportioning blame. In my experience, this is embraced wholeheartedly by other people whenever they would have been judged and found guilty.

I remember one time when I lent a book to a friend. She kept it for well over a year; eventually forgetting that she had it. When she remembered, she immediately contacted me and apologized profusely for keeping it for so long. She felt really bad about the inconvenience that she thought she had caused me. When I explained that there was no inconvenience – if I needed the book, I would have let her know, otherwise she was welcome to keep it – she felt completely relieved.

Unfortunately, the reverse is generally not true. While some people are prepared to reciprocate, many choose to judge me for my errors even while they appreciate not being judged for theirs. When I take the non-judgmental approach that I'm applying to them and extend it to myself as well, they see it as unwillingness to take responsibility for my mistakes.

A more accurate phrasing of this criticism is that it constitutes a deviation from the socially accepted form of accountability for one's conduct. This is true, though it is an open question whether the common form of accountability is in need of revision. This is not an easy question to answer in general, but we can and should decide which form of accountability we should use in our own lives instead of blindly adhering to the social norms. The burden of guilt that the social norms typically impose is sign enough that their re-examination is warranted.

Lack of Sensitivity in Painful Situations

This criticism has to do with the view that is at the heart of deliberate living, whereby every circumstance is seen as an opportunity for self-expression. It is not easy to reconcile this view with circumstances that are difficult or painful, especially if we are trying to make sense of this approach to living, having encountered it for the first time.

Whether the criticism is warranted depends on whether it is leveled in response to insensitive handling of a painful situation, or merely in anticipation of this. If the former, then the criticism is justified. If the latter, it is no more or less justified than the criticism of any other view that is open to misapplication.

For example, the belief that there is no life after death can be criticized on the same grounds, by accusing those who hold it of insensitivity – how can they be so cruel as to dash the hopes of people who have lost loved ones of ever seeing them again? However, the holding of such a belief doesn't mandate its insensitive application. A person who doesn't believe in an afterlife is not required to impose this view on other people while they are grieving or in any other situation at all. The potential for abuse exists, but so it does with every other conceivable belief.

Similarly, believing that every situation should be approached with the attitude of using it to fashion the most desirable experience doesn't require us to insist that other people do the same, especially in circumstances that are clearly difficult or painful. The pain must be healed first. Only then will people be in a position to consider what this approach to living has to offer, should we wish to make them aware of it.

Non-conformance

This is a more general formulation of the above criticisms. It can apply to every aspect of our lives that is normally affected by the need to conform to socially accepted behavior. The army is perhaps the most obvious example of social conformance. However, our daily lives are likely to abound with other, less prominent examples. These may range from our dress code and work hours to the very goals – in the form of wealth and status – that we are expected to set for ourselves.

Interestingly enough, non-conformance is not an explicit goal of deliberate living. Working towards this end actually interferes with the process. When it materializes, it is not because we are trying to complicate our lives by going against the grain, but simply because behaving according to the conventional wisdom is not the most satisfying approach in a particular situation.

It is the application of this process that has led me to deprioritize work from my life to where it was confined to regular working hours (I used to work overtime on regular basis), engage in recycling, compost our kitchen and garden waste, grow fruit trees, shrubs, vegetables and herbs in our garden, adopt a Jain diet, give away unneeded possessions, and make many other changes as well.

These decisions are decidedly at odds with the consumerist culture that is growing increasingly dominant in the society where I live. They follow from the examination of my relationship with other people and the environment and a choice of the desired experience in each context. That they constitute a rejection of much of the modern culture is incidental.[13]

When living life in this way, one can expect to encounter the full spectrum of reactions, from admiration to confusion, dismissal and even mobilization of defenses. It is important to realize that being true to our feelings can lead us away from what is considered normal behavior. People who are used to following social norms without subjecting them to significant scrutiny can easily find this threatening. Under-

---

[13] This reminds me of the famous statement by Mahatma Gandhi: "Be the change that you want to see in the world." It is interesting to note that, when a lifestyle is chosen based on adherence to an internal standard, it is worthwhile regardless of whether others follow suit.

standing the nature of this reaction can help us diffuse a potentially dangerous situation.

Living in a Dream World

This is a variation of the non-conformance criticism. By rejecting the popular values that we do not agree with, we can easily be perceived as trying to escape the reality of the larger society and live in a dream world of our own making. This is especially true if the values that we reject lie at the foundation of the modern society and are replaced with ideas that appear to be overly idealistic to be workable in the real world.

I think that this criticism is partially accurate. If we invest the time and the effort in examining how we feel about the situations that we come across in our daily lives, it will be all too easy to notice that a great deal of what transpires in the world today is not in agreement with our feelings. If we choose to honor our feelings and live in accordance with them, we will sometimes be compelled to act in ways that go against the social grain. In this sense, it would be accurate to say that deliberate living can easily lead to a partial rejection of the popular lifestyle.

The aspect of this criticism that is not accurate is the claim that this amounts to a withdrawal from reality and seeking refuge in fantasy. In order to make this claim, we have to assume that the world that we see around us – especially that which has been fashioned by us – is the reality and anything else is fantasy. This overlooks the fact that the world we live in is one of our own creations and requires continuous effort to maintain. We are always at liberty to choose a different vision and make that real.

Put another way, it seems to me that this claim is based on the assumption that our current social setup is relatively close to what we can reasonably hope to accomplish, and that rejection of it amounts to a refusal to come to terms with this fact. Any attempt to overhaul it, irrespective of scale, is therefore ill-conceived and doomed to failure.

This is a presumptuous claim. Social setups that work better than our modern one have already been utilized by some other cultures, particularly our hunter-gatherer ancestors. Furthermore, the modern lifestyle is not sustainable. Persevering with it can only lead to the demise of our civilization. It needs to be re-examined quite irrespective of whether a viable alternative has previously been found.

The process described in this book constitutes an attempt at creating a way of living and relating to the world around us that is in close agreement with our true nature, as revealed through our feelings. Adopting it should help us uncover ways of being that resonate with us more closely than our current lifestyle. Far from being a withdrawal from reality, this amounts to an attempt at remaking reality to what we genuinely want it to be.

Summary: Questions to Ask Myself

How do people react when I don't judge them for their actions? How do they respond when I don't judge myself for mine?

Can I tell when people want to know about my approach to life and when they don't? How do I avoid forcing my views on them when they are not wanted?

How much of my motivation for behaving in a certain way is external?

In a Nutshell

"If you can't explain it simply, you don't understand it well enough."
Albert Einstein

I'm a computer programmer by training. Having worked as a developer of business software for the past decade and pursued it as a hobby for another decade, I have become accustomed to formulating algorithms and drawing process flows. I find that they can be very effective at cutting through the detail to get to the very heart of the matter.

Because life itself is a process, I have chosen to present the content of the book in diagrammatic format. The purpose of this chapter is not to introduce new information, but to convey the core message with clarity, as per the above quote. Its usefulness lies in dispensing with all but the most essential ideas that have already been presented. As such, it shouldn't be used as a substitute for them, but merely as a means of putting them in perspective and defining their place in a larger context.

Subject Overview

The diagram serves as an overview of deliberate living as depicted in this book. I'm using the term *life elements* to refer to all our thoughts, words, actions, feelings, beliefs and circumstances. It is essentially a process of change from the way we are living now to the way we would ideally like to live. This involves three-fold change, represented by the three arrows on the diagram.

We need to work on our ability to intentionally bring about change in our lives in order to bring them closer to our ideal, until this ability encompasses everything that we can conceivably change. This is a domain of knowledge. Most of part two of the book is dedicated to exploring it, from the chapter Cultivating Awareness of Our Conduct all the way to the chapter Experimenting with Beliefs.

In addition to learning how to create the change that we seek, we need to cultivate our willingness to put that knowledge into practice. The necessity for this is introduced in the chapter The Placement of Responsibility and further explored in the chapters The Difficulty of Pursuing Deliberate Living and The Value of Attaining Deliberate Living from part three of the book. This is a domain of willingness or courage.

Still in the domain of courage, we need to be prepared to relinquish responsibility for changing things that reside outside of our control, as delineated by the bold block on the diagram. This is discussed in the section The Prudence of Discernment from the chapter Expanding Our Knowledge Base, as well as the section The Importance of Intention from the chapter When Things Fall Apart.

Ultimately, we want to be in a position where we drive the process of change instead of depending on the environment to force it upon us, are able to make the change that we seek, and have no need to change what lies outside of our control. The last point is exemplified by the goal that we are striving towards — living life as we have idealistically conceived it — being free from any elements that are not within our power to create.

The change itself is fuelled by the difference between the way we are currently living our lives and the way we would ideally want to live them. We identify this discrepancy by paying attention to our lives so that we can become fully aware of them, subjecting our observations to analysis in order to understand them, and evaluating them to ascertain their desirability. This informs our choice of life direction, which serves as a basis for our idea of how to live.

The idea of how we ought to be living is itself subject to change. As we grow and mature, so do our ideas of what is possible and what is worthwhile. This is explored in part one of the book, in the chapter <u>Key Concepts Pertaining to Deliberate Living</u>.

This leaves us in a position where we are making certain changes to our lives in an effort to bring them closer to our ideal, where those very changes cause a shift in the ideal that we are trying to achieve. We can still achieve it in certain situations, but on the whole, it lies beyond our grasp.

This can be disheartening if reaching the end of the journey is our goal. If, on the other hand, we are prepared to soften our gaze at the final destination to savor the burgeoning majesty of each passing step, we can rejoice in the knowledge that we have conceived of an even more magnificent state of being, and that, with time, it will grow into a vision that is grander still.

Living Deliberately

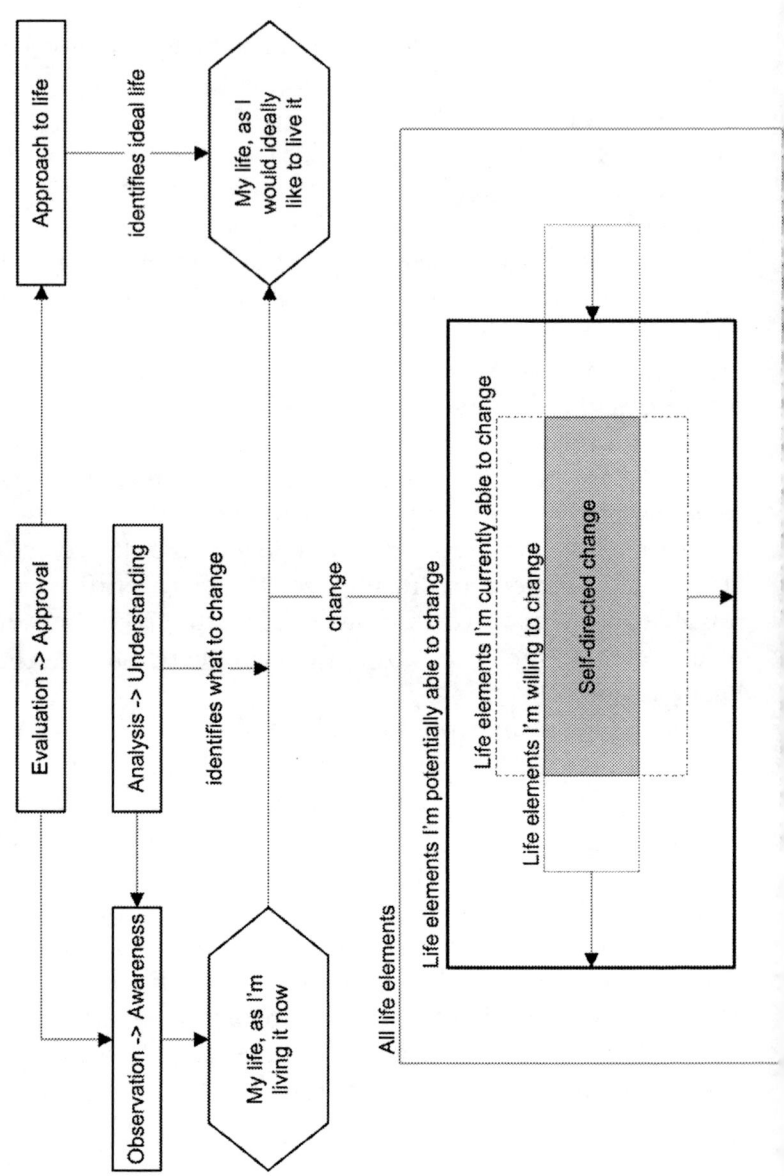

Generic Knowledge Base

I'm using the term *knowledge base* to refer to the repository of information on how to lead our lives that we have tucked away in our memories. It encompasses everything that we have discussed up to the chapter <u>Putting It All Together</u>.

Unlike the content of this book, the diagram has been phrased in question format. Its purpose is to highlight the important questions that need to be asked when deciding how to live our lives. It does not seek to provide answers to them. This exercise is left to the individual reader.

I've placed the approach to life at the base of the diagram because it doesn't really comprise a part of the knowledge base. Rather, it is the starting assumption that serves as the foundation on top of which the knowledge base is constructed. It tackles the question of what life is about, whereas the others deal with how to accomplish it. As such, we have to answer it before we can even decide which other questions we need to ask.

Hopefully the diagram makes it clear that the approach to living that is presented in this book is one of many that can be adopted. This makes it possible to tailor-make it to suit one's individual needs. A radically different set of questions can still provide useful guidance. The only requirement is that the approach provides practical, beneficial, and comprehensive guidelines for the living of one's life.

Living Deliberately

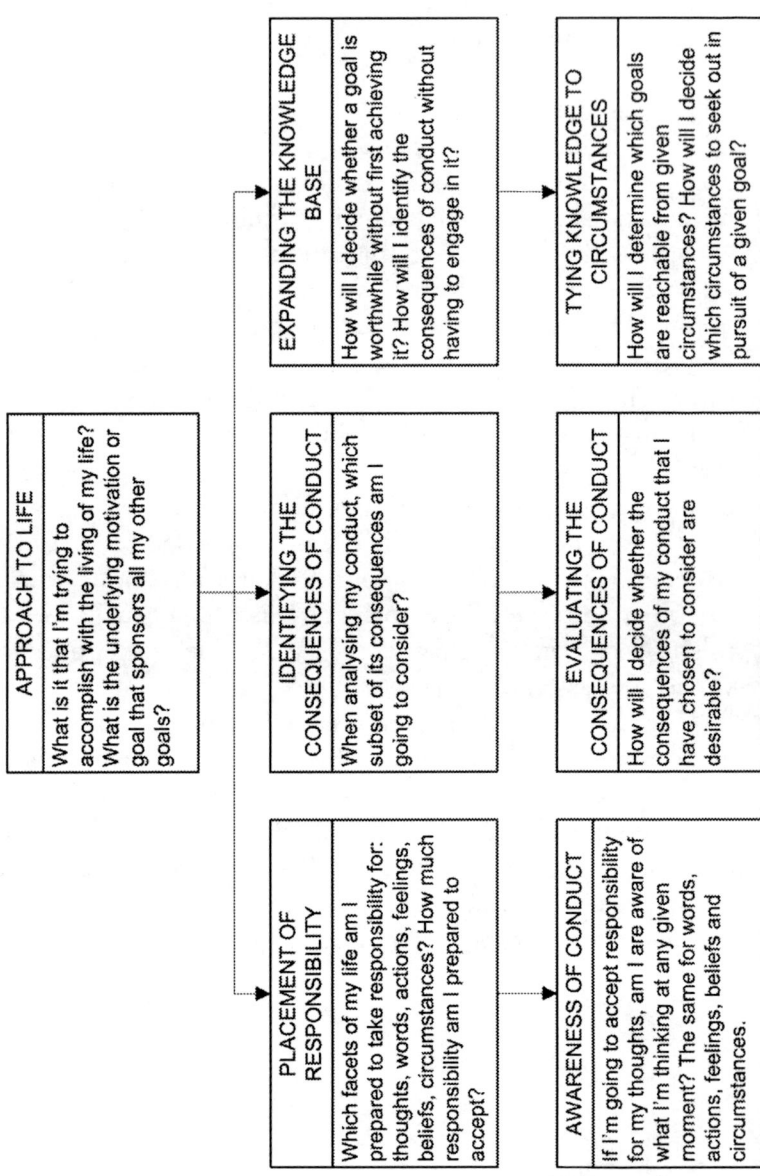

Personalized Knowledge Base

The following diagram takes the one from the previous section and answers its questions by drawing on the ideas presented in the book. It is intended as a concise summary of the covered material.

Again, these questions can be answered in a multitude of ways, depending on individual preferences. It would be a mistake to uncritically accept the answers that I've given. A much more beneficial approach would be to take the chosen set of guiding questions and derive your own answers, using the material from this and many other sources to stimulate your own personal search.

Living Deliberately

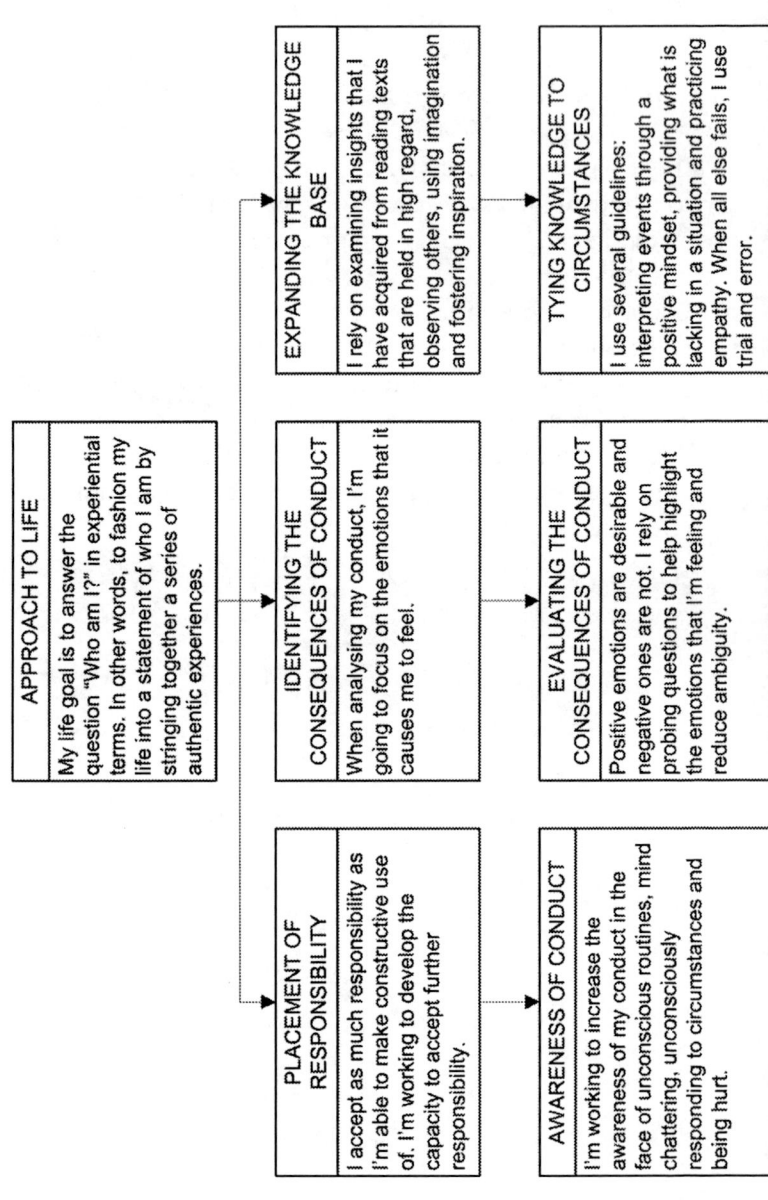

224

Beliefs

The diagram illustrates the process by which beliefs are typically adopted. Two distinct routes can be followed: we can either formulate beliefs on the basis of our personal experience, or uncritically accept the views that we are given by others.

There are two ways to validate beliefs that we've already adopted. Both rely on us acting in ways that demonstrate — via experience — more worthwhile alternatives. They work by focusing on the two highlighted blocks that sponsor behavior.

We can stimulate the change in behavior by disregarding the sponsoring influence of beliefs and acting on impulse instead. This approach is effective for beliefs that cannot be reconciled with radically different experience, as explained in the chapter <u>Identifying the Consequences of Our Conduct</u>.

For others, we have to intentionally adopt a different set of beliefs specifically for the purpose of guiding behavior. This approach is described in the chapter <u>Experimenting with Beliefs</u>.

Living Deliberately

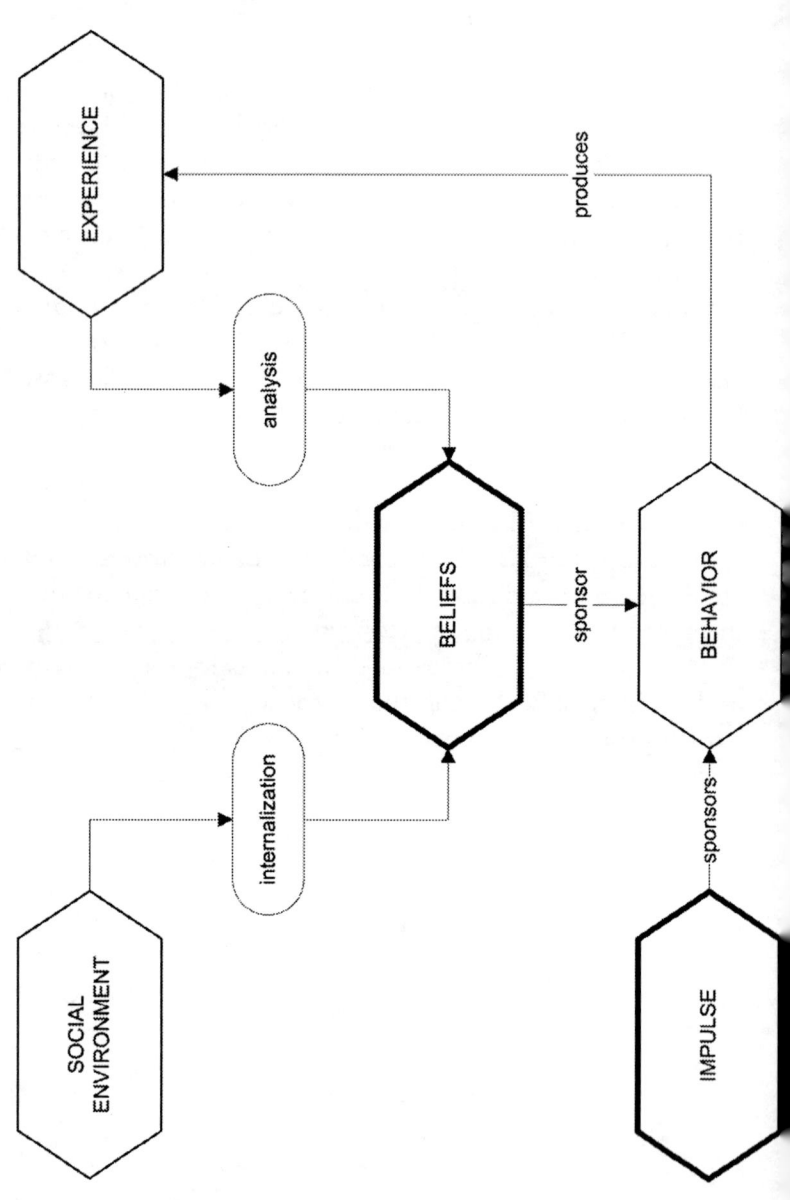

Decision Process

The decision process is depicted in the diagram below. It corresponds to the chapter <u>Putting It All Together</u>. The arrows indicate the direction in which the action takes place; for example, the *knowledge base* guides the *idealistic self-perception* and is extended by *analysis*.

Circumstances and *goals* are the starting points of the process – either we try to accomplish something given our circumstances, or we try to create specific circumstances given what we want to achieve.

Experience is the focal point of the whole process. The sole purpose of all the other steps is to enhance it. This follows from the answers that I've given in the previous section. Your answers may differ.

Living Deliberately

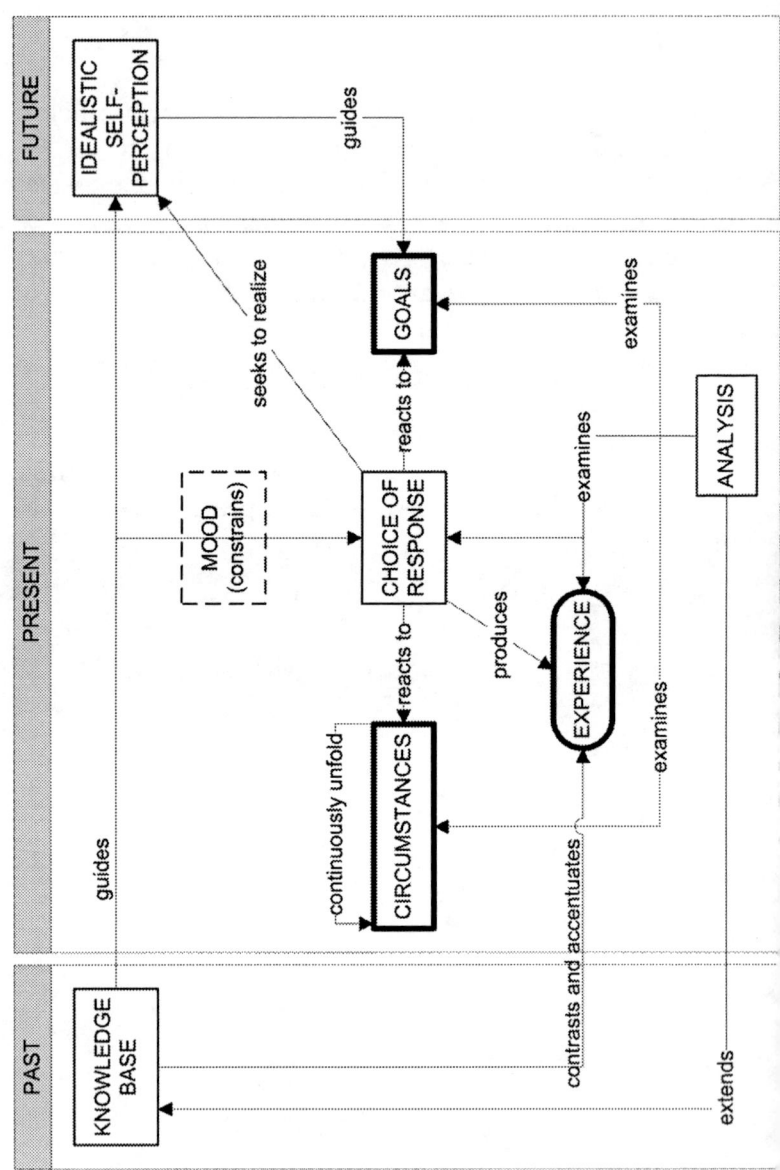

Hopefully the diagram is effective at conveying the never-ending cyclic nature of the process. While *circumstances* and *goals* are the natural starting points, it doesn't really matter where we become engaged in it; the feedback loops will soon force us to cover every step and lead us back to where we started. From there on, the cycle will replay itself over and over, for the remainder of our lives.

When we first start out on the journey to deliberate living, we might notice that the process flows erratically at times, and that our choices are influenced by our moods as much as by circumstances, goals, and means of achieving them. If so, then mastering the process will produce a stabilizing effect. As we identify the direction that we want it to go and make a concerted effort to steer it there, we will reduce the influence that our moods have on our conduct. Our behavior will gradually become what we truly wish it to be rather than what we couldn't help it being.

The process doesn't move forward by uncovering new steps, but by refining the few existing ones. The key to progress lies in continuous improvement of the idealistic self-perception. There are two factors that are primarily responsible for this.

Firstly, we need to become aware of ways of being that are superior to what we have sought to accomplish thus far. This is the subject of the chapter Expanding Our Knowledge Base. As we read about, observe or imagine behavior that leaves us so awed that we want to emulate it, we can use this information to improve our idealistic self-perception.

Secondly, edging closer to and especially achieving a state of being that we have set for ourselves gives us the confidence that we need to live life in this way. Failing to do this can easily cause us to draw a distinction between ourselves and our role models, where we perceive ourselves as inherently inferior to them and incapable of emulating their accomplishments. Success in this arena avoids the pitfall and sets our eyes firmly on the road ahead, confident that their example is firmly within our grasp and that it is only a matter of time before we are able to claim it as our own.

In Closing

I would like to take this opportunity to explode several myths that may have arisen during the reading of this book. Clinging onto them would diminish the value of its message and may even make it appear to be something that it is not.

The first myth is that I have mastered the approach to living, with all its nuances, that I've described in the book. I suppose this depends on what is meant by the word *master*. All of the insights that I've described, I've verified through personal experience. However, this doesn't mean that, once implemented, the process never goes astray. There are still numerous occasions when I forget to make use of the insights that I've described, fail at their application, or simply can't bring myself to apply them due to a counter-productive mindset.

This is not to say that improvements haven't been made. The pattern that I've noticed is that, once I become aware of a particular facet of my behavior that I wish to improve, I chip away at it so that the old behavior gradually manifests less frequently and only in more extreme circumstances. In this way, replacing it with more desirable behavior becomes a matter of habit.

These successes are partly obscured by the fact that, as I become more proficient at grappling with specific familiar challenges, I tend to become aware of new, more difficult ones. This is what leads me to believe that deliberate living is a journey of steady and lasting improvement that never runs out of challenges, no matter how many have already been overcome.

The second myth is that deliberate living is implemented as a matter of opinion. It may appear this way because the book follows a question-based approach and tries to avoid giving answers to those questions. This leaves it to the readers to give their own answers, which are invariably subjective in nature.

That answers are subjective doesn't make them a matter of personal taste. We cannot claim to live authentically if our answers are based on belief and opinion. Our choices amount to statements of preference, but preference for what we know to be true based on experience rather than what we pretend to be true via rationalization. Validating the choices that we make through personal experience takes them beyond opinion, belief, and the need for justification. They become facts.

The third myth is that the journey to deliberate living proceeds in an orderly fashion, following the sequence of steps laid out in this book. While there is a possibility that it may work out this way, and having access to the steps from the outset increases this possibility, my experience has been nothing like it.

Insights sprang up haphazardly in disparate parts of the process. I incorporated them as I grasped their significance and became able to relate to them. It took time for distinct steps to crystallize. In fact, I didn't even realize that I was dealing with a process that had concrete, discernable steps until a couple of years after I had engaged in it.

Even after the steps crystallized, new ones would occasionally come to the fore and existing ones would be seen in a new light – reinterpreted to where they performed a different function from the one that I had originally envisaged. Much like life itself that underwent periodic refinement in every sphere, the process that guided it was not exempt from exhibiting the same tendency.

Therein lies the strength of this approach to living. It is not like an academic qualification where one has to master the underlying theory before putting the concepts into practice. Progress can be made by paying attention to any of the details of the process described in this book. Practicing mindfulness can give us greater appreciation of the possibilities inherent in the present moment. Observing the behavior of other people can open our eyes to new ways of acting and being. Empathizing with them can help us understand them better. We don't need to place these things in a larger context to benefit from them. Doing so helps us make sense of the process and steer it in a desired direction, but it is not a prerequisite for making any progress at all.

And the last myth is that the process of continuous growth and improvement described in the book comes to occupy the central place in one's life. It does not. It is not an end in itself. It is a tool to a greater end. As much as a sculptor may appreciate the fine tools that enable him to do his work and the finely honed skills with which to use them, it is their application in the shaping of a sculpture that holds his attention.

Within the context of this book, that sculpture consists of the series of experiences that comprise our lives. We shape them by the deft application of the concepts and principles associated with deliberate living. These tools and skills are priceless. Without them, we might not even realize that what we are doing is chipping away stone or connect one such act with another. Nevertheless, as precious as they are, it is their application to produce experience that is central to our existence. It is this experience that I would call the essence of life.

There is satisfaction to be had in looking back at an event and recognizing our idealistic self-perception fully realized in our conduct. It is fulfilling to watch our reaction to circumstances and recognize that we have handled them better than on any previous attempt. Our life contains moments of indescribable beauty where we experience ourselves as the kind, loving, caring and compassionate people that we know ourselves to be. It is my hope that the insights presented in this book will help us increase the incidence of these moments until they permeate our lives.

Nowadays, when I ponder what it is that I want out of life, I tend to settle for being able to recognize myself in my memories. I wish the same to you.

Where to from here?

"The important work of moving the world forward does not wait to be done by perfect men."

George Eliot

Because the book is essentially an overview of the many subjects that contribute to deliberate living, it is not intended to be the final word on any of them. This role is deferred to the more specialized books and other works written by experts in their respective fields. Some of them have been mentioned in footnotes at the relevant sections of this book.

The purpose of this section is to bring the material together for ease of reference, and to suggest the next leg of the journey.

Acquiring Further Insights

Perhaps the most appropriate place to start is with the series of books that have marked the turning point in my life and have set me on the way to deliberate living. These are the *Conversations with God* books by Neale Donald Walsch. They do a masterful job of tackling some of the same subjects that are discussed in this book.

Despite its academic jargon, Jenny Wade's book *Changes of Mind: A Holonomic Theory of the Evolution of Consciousness* is very thorough at describing authentic consciousness, which is the level of consciousness associated with deliberate living. Because her theory is comprehensive – it encompasses consciousness from prenatal to after-death stages – it is also very effective at contrasting authentic consciousness with that from other stages.

Hazrat Inayat Khan's book *Personality: The Art of Being and Becoming* is a rare example of a mystic bringing his insights to bear on living in the mundane world. There is a considerable overlap between its subject matter and this book, though written from a different perspective.

In the book *Learned Optimism: How to Change Your Mind and Your Life*, Martin Seligman tackles the difficult subject of cultivating a positive mindset with which to face adversity. Drawing on his background in psychology and clinical research, he offers explanations and guidelines that are well supported by scientific studies.

The Miracle of Mindfulness by Thich Nhat Hanh delivers both the beauty and the depth of the practice of mindfulness. This is extended by Casey Blood in the book *Science, Sense & Soul: The Mystical-Physical Nature of Human Existence* to examine various other meditation techniques.

Even though John Perkins and Alice Walker are quoted for examples of beliefs and behavior of people from other cultures, the two books that I have found the most informative in this regard are *Other Ways of Knowing: Recharting Our Future with Ageless Wisdom* by John Broomfield, and *Original Wisdom: Stories of an Ancient Way of Knowing* by Robert Wolff.

Further insights can be acquired by reading other written material, such as magazine articles and Internet blog entries. It might be worthwhile to subscribe to a magazine that is devoted to personal growth. I have found the Sacred Journey journal (http://www.fellowshipinprayer.com) both informative and inspiring.

With its extensive cross referencing and powerful search capability, the Internet has become a very useful resource on a wide variety of subjects. It often surpasses books with availability, and, sometimes, even quality of information.

Inspiration can also be stimulated in numerous ways. The most popular of these are various forms of meditation and yoga, but they can even encompass the likes of hypnosis and ingesting psychedelic substances. It is not necessary to go to these lengths in search of insight, however. We can simply identify what relaxes, awes, and inspires us and make space for it in our lives. This could consist of admiring art, walking through the woods, watching the sunset or the stars, dream imagery, or simply silence. The last one is particularly difficult to come by with the constant milling of people and humming of electrical appliances that punctuate the modern urban landscape.

Living the Insights

Applying the insights that we have gathered is closely tied to part three of this book. Once we have acquired the knowledge that enables us to live deliberately, putting it into practice becomes a matter of resolve. It stems from the inner drive for a purposeful existence, bolstered by the beneficial effects that arise from this kind of lifestyle.

I have found it immeasurably useful to associate with other people who are on a similar journey. We share our goals and aspirations, the methods for reaching them, and the successes and failures that result. We don't necessarily agree on which steps to take, but we can nevertheless explore them together and support each other along the way.

It is essentially about engaging with people who are moved by the same questions in life. These questions stand in stark contrast to the questions that pertain to income and social status that feature prominently in our society. Having this support structure helps maintain our focus on the largest questions in life so that it is not drowned out by the countless mundane activities that vie for our attention.

On a larger scale, it may be useful to join organizations that have been founded specifically for this purpose. This role is most commonly played by religious organizations, even though their search is typically constrained by a rigid belief system. Purely spiritual organizations – such as Self Knowledge Symposium (http://www.selfknowledge.org) – also exist, but are comparatively rare.

Social Activism

Living the insights brings us into the social domain. In my experience, there is a yawning gulf between human life lived at the height of its potential and human life as prescribed by our society. I have touched on the difference in the chapter The Difficulty of Pursuing Deliberate Living.

This raises the dilemma of how to respond to a society that has been erected on an alien set of values. Some people attempt to escape its constraints by forming small communities on its outskirts where they can live on their own terms.

Others remain within its folds and carve out a niche for themselves where they can be relatively true to their own values within the larger framework of the societal ones. For me, the authentic response is to change the society.

Changing society is in some ways unavoidable. We impact people around us by virtue of associating with them. We don't have to take to the streets, banners in hand, to influence the world in which we live. It is sufficient that we be true to ourselves instead of societal norms in simple, everyday matters – how much time we dedicate to our intellectual and spiritual nourishment, how we relate to the people around us, the choice of food that we eat, how we dispose of our waste, and so on. Duane Elgin's landmark book *Voluntary Simplicity* contains a very informative overview of these changes, as described by the people who have made them.

Those of us who wish to play a more active role in social activism can explore numerous projects and initiatives that are presently underway. They are the work of individuals and organizations that are likewise disenchanted with the present state of affairs and see the need for change. Most of them have a relatively localized focus. Even though humanitarian and environmental activities attract the bulk of media attention, the work of these organizations is actually very diverse.

Some play an educational role, either by freely sharing information on a wide variety of subjects, or on specific topics. Some others are concerned with reorganizing our lifestyles, typically with the eye to strengthening social bonds. There are also concerted attempts to localize or even eliminate currency, check the retributive tendencies of our judiciary, and many others. Together, they cover all aspects of our society.

Contributing to one or more of these initiatives would certainly help bring about the much needed change. A comprehensive listing can be found at Wiser Earth (http://www.wiserearth.org). It contains a directory of more than 110,000 non-governmental and socially responsible organizations that are active in 243 countries.

Based on my interaction with social activists who are committed to specific projects, I've come to realize that their work could be aided considerably by supplying two more ingredients – self-knowledge with its wider social implications, and a clear understanding of where specific initiatives fit into the overall scheme of social transformation.

I have started a project in an attempt to provide both of these. It aims to foster personal development and use the resulting self-knowledge to deduce features of society that we would ideally like to live in. It also strives to describe the transition process from the current society to the idealistic one. It identifies organizations and projects that are associated with each step and shows how they complement one another to bring about widespread change.

Ultimately, my goal is to create what I call a self-reflective society – a society that is built on the principles of deliberate living as described in this book.

The Self-Reflective Society project can be found at http://selfreflectivesociety.org.

It is still in its infancy at the time of this writing. A great deal of useful information on each facet of the project can still be provided. If you see value in this work, please join me in making a self-reflective society a reality.

Summary: Quick Reference

Acquiring Further Insights:
- *Conversations with God* series of books by Neale Donald Walsch
- *Changes of Mind: A Holonomic Theory of the Evolution of Consciousness* by Jenny Wade
- *Personality: The Art of Being and Becoming* by Hazrat Inayat Khan
- *Learned Optimism: How to Change Your Mind and Your Life* by Martin Seligman
- *The Miracle of Mindfulness* by Thich Nhat Hanh
- *Science, Sense & Soul: The Mystical-Physical Nature of Human Existence* by Casey Blood
- *Other Ways of Knowing: Recharting Our Future with Ageless Wisdom* by John Broomfield
- *Original Wisdom: Stories of an Ancient Way of Knowing* by Robert Wolff
- Sacred Journey journal (http://www.fellowshipinprayer.com)

Living the Insights:
- Self Knowledge Symposium (http://www.selfknowledge.org)

Social Activism:
- *Voluntary Simplicity: Toward a Way of Life That Is Outwardly Simple, Inwardly Rich* by Duane Elgin
- Wiser Earth (http://www.wiserearth.org)
- Self-Reflective Society (http://selfreflectivesociety.org)

Acknowledgments

Many of the ideas discussed in this book were taken from the Conversations with God series of books by Neale Donald Walsch. Having experimented with them for several years with good results, I decided to collate them under the banner of deliberate living. In so doing, I supplemented them with ideas that were not contained in these books, or were mentioned too briefly for a reader to easily appreciate their significance. I also expanded on them, using examples from my life to highlight the finer points, as well as from the lives of many people who have contributed to the material presented in this book.

I'm exceedingly grateful to the people who have shared in my life journey that followed the reading of the Conversations with God books. These include not only family and friends, but also people I've met over the Internet. This is especially true of members of the Internet discussion forums, particularly the folks at the Alternative Religions section of the Free Thought & Rationalism Discussion Board, that I have participated in over the years. Their insights into living have certainly enriched my own.

I would like to thank all of the people who have directly contributed to the material presented in this book, particularly Julio Carrancho and Tony Bevan for their willingness to edit what was essentially a stranger's manuscript. The time and the effort that they've put in are warmly appreciated. Most of all, I would like to thank my editor, Chantól Sego, for her uncompromising commitment to quality. Her penetrating insights have certainly helped make the message of the book much more accessible.

About the Author

Hrvoje Butković was born in 1974 in Croatia, then Yugoslavia. He immigrated with his family to South Africa when he was 14 years old. This proved to be an auspicious move, with the Yugoslavian civil war breaking out the following year. He currently lives in Johannesburg, South Africa, with his wife and two children.

For more information about his work, including regular updates, please visit http://fluffygroovy.com.